LAUNCHING!

LAUNCHING!
Jeffrey Hugh Newman

Walnut Road Press

© 2014 Jeffrey Hugh Newman

Printed and bound in the United States of America. All rights reserved. No part of this publication may be reproduced or transmitted in any form or by any means, electronic or mechanical, including photocopying, recording, or by an information storage and retrieval system—except by a reviewer who may quote brief passages in a review to be printed in a magazine, newspaper, or on the Web—without permission in writing from the publisher.

Published in the United States by
Walnut Road Press LLC
One Riverfront Plaza, 11th Floor
Newark, New Jersey 07102

ISBN: 978-0615922041

10 9 8 7 6 5 4 3 2 1

IN MEMORIAM

To my beloved son,

,

to whom this book is dedicated.

May the world overflow with young men like Jon who was a great son to me and his mother, a great husband to Angella and a great father to Aviva and Ayla.

Jon's kindness, love, warmth, and maturity beyond his years is a source of inspiration to all who knew him.

Perhaps the true measure of anyone's time on this Earth is how others perceived him. Jon was considered by each and every one of his friends as their single best friend – a true hallmark of a life well spent and beautifully lived.

He was my best friend, too.

ACKNOWLEDGMENTS

The first acknowledgement belongs to the Creator ... my books have been "in me" for years, but He allowed me the pleasure and fulfillment of sharing it with others. This has given me the opportunity to make an impression on the lives of others, howsoever insignificant. To allow me to feel that I am somehow giving back ... I will always be grateful.

I thank the many people who have made an imprint on my life. I have been blessed. My first wife, Linda, who is one of the kindest people I know. My second wife, Sheryl, who died from cancer. She was one of the most graceful persons I have yet to know. She brought out the best in everyone she touched.

My parents, Mark and Gloria, my brother, Mark, and my children, Alyssa and Jon, each of whom, in entirely different ways, have had varying positive impacts on my growth and development.

Michael Kercheval and his incredible staff at the International Council of Shopping Centers, all of whom trusted me, and trust me to participate as a speaker at many of their events and as a leader of several committees.

Patricia Karetsky, who catalyzed me to start writing by advising it only requires an hour a day, and Ron Pompei, who constantly assured me that I had something worthwhile to communicate.

Victoria Wright, who constantly challenged me to write better, make my work clearer, make it "sing."

All of my friends and colleagues, who, in a variety of everyday little ways, helped me to grow, learn to laugh with myself, accept myself and appreciate myself.

Steven Gross, Chairman of my law firm, who has been both a friend and mentor, not just to me, but to all of my partners. Max Crane, Managing Partner of my law firm, for his continuing support of my efforts in creating my books. Both true leaders.

I am especially thankful to all of my muses. How lucky and grateful am I to have multiple muses. My fiancée, Barbara. My colleague, Marcia, my colleague, Patrick, who created the graphic designs, my terrific former assistant, Celeste, and my terrific current assistant, Carolyn.

Special thanks to my super motivators ... my grandchildren, Lia, Ari, Aviva, Eli, and Ayla.

Lastly, to all those who have come before me with self-help and other motivational works. I seek not to stand on their shoulders; rather, to someday perhaps stand shoulder-to-shoulder.

Table *of* Contents

Forward 1

Chapter 1
BRANDING 3

Chapter 2
PRESENCE 9

Chapter 3
THE FEAR OF SELF-NEGOTIATION 15

Chapter 4
**MARKETING FOR LAWYERS
(AND OTHER PROFESSIONALS)** 25

Chapter 5
ORGANIZATIONAL MARKETING 35

Chapter 6
**MARKETING
(TIMELINESS AND COMMUNICATION)** 43

Chapter 7
THE ZEN OF COLONY 49

Chapter 8
THE NEGOTIATION OF MOTIVATION 59

Chapter 9
NEGOTIATION "WARM-UPS" 69

Chapter 10
THE CLOSING 77

Chapter 11
NEGOTIATING TECHNIQUES – FOR LEADERS AND THEIR LAWYERS – ATTITUDE AND FOCUS 85

Chapter 12
NEGOTIATING TECHNIQUES – FOR LEADERS AND THEIR LAWYERS – PREPARATION 93

Chapter 13
NEGOTIATING TECHNIQUES – FOR LEADERS AND THEIR LAWYERS – TACTICS 103

Chapter 14
NEGOTIATING TECHNIQUES – FOR LEADERS AND THEIR LAWYERS – MIDDLE AND ENDGAME GAMBITS 111

Chapter 15
THE TRIPLE PLAY 121

Notes 127

FORWARD

Professionals dedicate their school lives to learning a profession. They are taught the substantive knowledge necessary to be smart lawyers, doctors, and accountants. Yet, there are scant few, if any, courses teaching the skills and techniques of marketing, leadership and negotiation. This book, the third in a trilogy, will improve these skills and fuse the underlying tools and principles that need to be mastered in order to succeed, not just as a bright professional, but also—on an even higher level—as an effective marketer, leader and negotiator. What is needed is, simply, focus and practice. All of these can be mastered sufficiently to allow every professional to enhance performance.

Each chapter addresses one or more skills, techniques, and principles, and the methods of acquiring, enhancing, and honing them. Perhaps not surprisingly, most of the skills, techniques, and principles focused upon and developed throughout the book form a common foundation and are exhibited by all successful marketers, leaders and negotiators. By employing the principles and techniques laced throughout this book, you will enhance and improve your practice. I am confident you will agree.

Chapter 1
BRANDING

LAUNCHING!

How do we brand ourselves? Whether we realize it or not, we are creating and/or adjusting our brand almost every day.

In short, our brand is the amalgamation of the way we interact with others in all of our interpersonal relationships. Each interaction is a building block in the development and construction of how we present ourselves to the world. Our brand can tarnish as a result of a graceless interaction. We all have had bad moments and bad days. But if the overall presentation of who we are is positive and graceful, we can easily remove the tarnish of a "bad moment." Everyone cannot like us. Yet, our brand becomes a function of what others think of us and how they perceive us. Because we act and react differently in varying situations and in different ways with different people, we need to think of our brand as the common denominator of the way in which most think of us and the way in which most react and respond to us. A bad interaction is so easy to neutralize, or even to change to a positive after-moment. Apologies generally do the trick!

While we don't expect everyone to like us, we all wish that most do. More important, in a work context, we want others to respect us and feel comfortable that they can rely on us.

How do we create and enhance a positive perception in others about us? What is required of us to gain the respect of others and to gain their confidence? Our brand grows positively like a tree grows in height. Yet, it can collapse and fall at the speed a tree falls.

While it would be terrific if we all could develop a new life-saving vaccine, or otherwise develop novel and successful solutions to real problems facing others, it's not necessary. In fact, few of us will achieve that type of success, or that type of fame.

But fame is not necessary to create our brand. In fact, no big accomplishments are necessary. So what does it take? All it takes is our consistently good performance handling the little things, the things of which every day life is composed. Let's analyze several of the little things that occur virtually every day.

For example, how do we respond to a person—our child, our spouse, our colleague—who interrupts us to ask a question or obtain some advice? We are always thinking. Perhaps we are ruminating about trivialities, or an upcoming encounter, or even recalling a painful or exhilarating past event. When someone approaches us and says more than a perfunctory "Hello, how are you?" the encounter becomes an interruption. It requires our focus.

So let's say our thoughts are deep and focused when someone starts to engage us in a conversation. How do we respond? How often is our response, "I can't talk to you right now—I'm in the middle of something?" How often do we allow ourselves to be interrupted but attempt to short-circuit the encounter? We may say, "Can I catch you later?" Or our facial expressions may broadcast our lack of interest. On the other hand, how often do we allow the interruption to "take hold," discontinue our rumination, and focus, really focus, on not just the spoken words of the other person, but on the other person's entire being?

Let's assume you are really busy, pressured by a deadline and, worse yet, behind schedule. Why not give the person interrupting you sixty seconds to speak. Is this too much? How about giving them thirty seconds, or a scant fifteen seconds? Doesn't sound like much—it isn't—but it will feel like a lifetime when you are under pressure. In that period of time, deliver the entirety of your focus to what the person

LAUNCHING!

interrupting you is saying. By the end of the fifteen seconds—which will feel interminable—you will be able to absorb and analyze the input you need. You will learn:

- Is the interruption a trivial conversation?

- Does the person interrupting have a real problem or issue to discuss?

- Can you help?

- How much time will it take to help?

At that point, you can determine whether to let the interruption take hold, suggest a meeting at a later time when you can properly vet the problem, or determine whether someone else can help instead, due to your deadline.

What have you accomplished for your brand? Studies show that allowing someone to speak without interruption for at least fifteen seconds telegraphs respect and concern. At that point, your brand can allow the interruption to continue or defer or deflect the interruption. A fifteen-second focus is more due than most interrupters will get when the person they are interrupting is preoccupied.

How good are you at living in the present moment, and embracing the other person with your full energy of attention? The attention of your ears as you listen, the attention of your eyes as you observe, and the attention of your entire being can work to absorb all the communication signals the other person is sending.

Which response is likely to improve your brand? Whether it's likeability or respect for others or concern for others, don't we want to constantly polish each of these?

Of course we do, especially if it's in our role as parent, spouse, sibling, or co-worker. It's not about the birthday present for your child, or the fabulous night out with your spouse, or your brotherly or sisterly concern, or your brilliant idea at work. It's about the little, every-day interactions that truly define who we are. The interactions that are an annoyance, an interruption or even upsetting to us because our child wants a curfew extension or our spouse no longer wants to see the movie you agreed upon, or your sibling is unable to take your parent to the doctor and needs you to fill in, or your colleague just needs you as a sounding board.

Branding is built on a daily basis by the manner in which we interact with others. There's no point in buying sixty seconds of television commercial time or a highway billboard to extol our virtues and how wonderful we are. We don't need it and it won't work. Fortunately, there's all the time to do so on a bit-by-bit, everyday basis by dealing with others with grace and respect, no matter who they are (insignificant or not, in our minds) or what they want.

Here is another example. Have you ever responded to a question either with words, or that oh-so-obvious look of disdain? Why? Probably your insecurity or your anger toward the other person or an unrelated person for a past insult (whether correctly perceived or not) caused you to demean the other person. What did you accomplish? If nothing else, you snipped off a tiny little piece of your positive brand. But, make no mistake about it, with enough snips, the garment changes its look and can even become unfit to wear.

Let's take another less obvious, almost insidious, type of interaction that tarnishes our brand. When you are asked to perform a task, such as clean the garage, pick up the cleaning, or take on a new assignment at work, what is your immediate and initial response? How often do you say, "Yes, I'll get right on it"? And, how often do you say, "I'll get to it if I can," or "I'm not sure I can get to it for X days," or simply, "Maybe"?

For which response do you want to be known? Obviously, we all want others to know we can be relied on and get the job done. Yet, our insecurity or our current focus sometimes causes us to respond conditionally. A response with an "if" or a "maybe" or an "I'll try" or an "I'll see," is a conditional response undercutting any sense of certainty.

LAUNCHING!

It undermines the reliance the other person seeks. It undermines your brand of "you can count on me."

Ironically, even if you perform after an initial tepid response, the luster of the performance is diminished. It's diminished because of the lack of absolute and timely certainty of completing the performance by virtue of the initial equivocal response. And, if we undercut our performance with "Maybe" and "I'll try," we must surely be undermining our brand. We diminish ourselves and our brand by failing to present ourselves as a can-do person—instead, branding ourselves as a "you-never-know-for-sure" person.

We brand ourselves almost every day. Each encounter constitutes yet another tiny building block in the mosaic of our brand of who we are. Build your brand of a graceful and reliable "I will," and work every day to enhance that perception of you by others.

Do this, because, as we all know, each person's perception is his or her reality. Their image of you is "their you."

PRACTICE POINTS

- What is your brand? What do you project?

- Be positive. Attitude is everything.

- Be an "I can," "I will" person.

- Never be an "I'll try" or "If only" person.

- Do not (intentionally) put others on the defensive.

- Use words and expressions that imply "tell me more."

Chapter 2
PRESENCE

LAUNCHING!

How do you make people feel? Have you ever really thought about how people feel? Why should you care? You should care. Surprisingly perhaps, the way you feel about others is generally the way they feel about you. It's not psychological, it's physical. It's the boomerang effect of the verbal and nonverbal cues you emit.

In one of my prior books, I discussed an encounter between two colleagues, one much more senior than the other. The junior colleague was meeting with his superior to report on a matter they were working on together. The junior colleague was a young lawyer, but he could have been a child, a spouse, or a fellow church member. Because the scenario was in the report context, I focused on techniques to elicit a full report from the subordinate, uncovering not just the good news, but also the bad. If you read that book, you'll enjoy re-discovering the techniques that act as a poultice to draw out problems besetting a deal you are transacting with your colleague or school issues your child is facing.

However, now we will focus on our presence: the demeanor we exhibit, the vibrations we send, our aura. Why? Because we are what we project, and what we project sets the tone for the encounter.

Have you ever sat in the audience waiting for a speaker or a performer (it could also be a loved one, colleague or adversary)? As the person began, did your emotions rise or fall? Did the performer or presenter give off a positive energy? Did you immediately feel a sense of connection? Or, did you feel a sense of letdown that you sought to fight off, hoping the presentation would improve? What presence did they bring to the performance? Was it that of a high-energy entertainer or was it the antithesis, the demeanor of an internally focused guitarist or cellist emitting the closed presence of a performer solely focused on his instrument, almost playing for himself, as he sought to bring the sounds of his instrument to a level of perfection only he could perhaps truly appreciate?

What brand of presence do you seek to emit? A desire to connect? A desire to understand? A sense of reaching out to create an interpersonal engagement? Or, on the other hand, do you display a sense of aloofness, distraction or, worse, complete lack of interest? Of course, the bigger question is, do you know how the other person is reacting, and could you be sabotaging the positive result you seek to create and obtain from the encounter?

How do we sabotage ourselves? We do so in many ways, some intentional and others unintentional. Perhaps the most common form of sabotage is our inability to really listen—to be in the present moment and focus on what the other person is saying. When we do focus, we give off the energy of respect that comes from truly trying to understand the other person.

But to do so is hard. It requires us to drop all else on our mind so we can really listen. Listen with our ears, our eyes, our entire being. How can we do that if we interrupt, if we are distracted, and most important, if we don't ask questions and confirm not what we think we heard but what we think the other person was trying to communicate?

What is it that we radiate and does it match what we want to radiate? How can we know if we don't listen to the other person? We need to listen to not just his words but his inflection, tone, cadence and rhythm and, most important, his posture and body movement: the sum of all of his responses, verbal and nonverbal.

Perhaps you will not be surprised when I tell you that the nonverbal responses often present the true "tells" of how others are receiving you. All of us tend to be able to control our words—it's the rest of our communication conduits that are less easily controlled. Hence, the

LAUNCHING!

folded arms, the little step back, the slight grimace or pursing of the lips, or the rise of volume quickly caught and subdued by the speaker.

When we pay attention to the little things, we can gauge the way in which our presence, our vibes, our demeanor, and our aroma is being perceived. We all feel each other's energy, whether we realize it or not. Each of us is a collection of atoms and as each of us "bumps" into each other, just like atoms, we either emit energy, positive or negative, or we absorb it. Emitters are almost always more likely to succeed; absorbers can be successful contemplative thinkers but they can also become like a black hole taking energy out of a meeting, even out of an entire room, and never releasing it.

So we want to be motivators and we want to emit positive vibrations. How do we do it, especially on those difficult days filled with our own issues and problems not easily resolved? It's easy. We compartmentalize. Think of your demeanor as your attitude at that moment. The little secret is that a bad day needn't be a bad day that infuses your every waking moment. Treat your attitude as piece of clothing. If it's soiled, change it. It's that easy, and it will work if you let it. You'll have plenty of time to return to those taxing issues and problems. But for now focus on the person or group before you and let your electrons fly! Let's see. Have you ever started a day fretting over a dental appointment scheduled after work? Perhaps you made the appointment because of a nagging toothache, and you are fearful that it may require a root canal procedure and not just a filling. Will you allow that anxiety to infect your entire day and your conversations and meetings that day, or will you block it out, compartmentalize it, and conduct yourself in your normal positive manner? Select the second option—always. What's the point in allowing a future event over which you have no control to negatively infect your entire day? No matter how you act during the day, it won't change the outcome of the dental visit. So put the anxiety in the back of your mind and conduct yourself in your normal kind and graceful manner—compartmentalize. Don't fall into the "woe is me" trap allowing you to justify a negative attitude, surly tone, or off-putting gesture.

Create a smile by giving a smile. Confer respect by paying attention. Don't let your mind wander—others can tell. Focus on one encounter at a time. Multi-tasking is misunderstood. It's not performing multiple tasks simultaneously. It's performing multiple tasks in the same overall time frame, but focusing on each separately, one at a time. We must force ourselves to be in the present moment with each task we perform.

If we are not in the present moment, then we are dwelling on the past or dreaming about the future. Those vibrations swirl inside of us and can not be absorbed by the person in front of us. Those vibrations don't leave us; even if they do, they dissipate into space. No connection can be made unless we focus and direct our energy and vibrations directly at each other. Think and live in each "now"—each existential moment. Your presence will thank you and your encounters will improve.

PRACTICE POINTS

- Be in the present. Maintain focus!

- When we daydream, we telegraph our desire to be somewhere else.

- When we daydream, we are only partially present.

- We all have baggage. Learn to put your valises away, just for the duration of that meeting.

Chapter 3
THE FEAR OF SELF-NEGOTIATION

LAUNCHING!

Fear can be a motivator. On the other hand, fear can be a chiller and freeze us. In either case, fear pushes us to the edges of who we are—either accelerating our actions or freezing us into a state of inaction. In either case fear pushes us to extremes, a place we would never elect to be.

Yet, fear is a basic human emotion. On Wall Street it is often said that fear and greed are the two antithetical motivators for trading. In fact, quantitative analysts, "quants," use algorithms to plot fear. By so doing, they can create trading models that can take advantage of periods of high fear.

They do so by plotting fear levels and using sophisticated trading techniques during those periods of elevated anxiety. By creating programs that recognize periods of elevated fear, their computers execute trades when fear is highest. Perhaps not surprisingly, because the programs are essentially executed by machines, they do not react to the fear levels. Hence, these so called quant traders often do best during high levels of fear.

Similarly, many traders and investors become infected by the news headlines of the day. There are always problems in the world, yet somehow the market nevertheless goes up and down during times when world events seem bleak and/or foreboding. But following the news seldom seems to be instructive for traders and investors. Is it the fear or elation that the headlines induce that is the basis for the bromide that the public tends to sell at the bottom and buy at the top?

Is it any different for any of us in any business? We must always be on guard against our fear. It is always lurking inside of us, looking

Chapter 3 | THE FEAR OF SELF-NEGOTIATION

for the opportunity to fester, surface, and grow, and infect our thought processes, creating an anxiety within us about all our decisions.

What must we constantly do to suppress and neutralize our fear? Get the facts, visualize, and internalize possible outcomes. Do our best and recognize we can live with that result. Now, I'm not talking about the fear that arises from being unprepared; nor am I talking about the fear of falling off if we stand too close to the edge of a cliff. Those emotions are positive fear.

I am talking about the fear of the unknown, the unknown outcome from a considered, but new, course of action, or the unknown response from a superior or a client to the admission of a mistake. It is these fears that bring us to the edge—to our extremes—the extremes of "frenzy or freeze." We may try to hide our mistake by nondisclosure, or accelerate our response and make a series of quick, ill-judged actions to fix the mistake before it's uncovered. What we should do is gather all the facts and calmly and rationally elect a course of action based on them.

Returning to the stock market analogy, what do the best traders and investors do in stressful situations? They filter out the background noise. They realize that events change by the hour and new events crop up daily. They know that the best decisions are made with the facts, usually not in the midst of a trading room, but in the self-illuminating light from their own reflection while thinking things through in silence.

What do the enlightened traders and investors do? First, they analyze the price movements and volume changes of their target stock. That information often provides valuable clues about investor interest and belief in a company. Second, they analyze a company's fundamentals, balance sheet, profit-and-loss statements, and so on, together with the stock's short, intermediate and long-term chart patterns. Third, they most likely ignore just about everything else. Why?

Because, facts and patterns provide the "tell." Beyond the screaming headlines of the day, and the emotional positive or negative exhortations of others, the facts, and the patterns of behavior, remain the overwhelmingly vital clues. It's the same in business. Fear trumps

LAUNCHING!

brains unless the brains are armed with the facts and the patterns of behavior. Yet, many of us allow so many of our decisions to be affected by fear. It's insidious. We don't even realize it. Let's see.

We arrive at work at 8:00 a.m. to realize that we have more to do than we originally thought. An emergency patient, a client with a crisis, an unanticipated meeting we must attend that day—any number of unexpected intrusions create the tension of that "not enough time in the day" feeling. As a result, we start the day a bit off-kilter, not sure we can get everything accomplished.

This type of day can develop in one of three ways. We can push through all the projects we feel we must complete by prioritizing and accelerating our actions. Or, if anxiety really takes hold, we can either rush the projects or we can freeze up and struggle to complete any project. For most of us, unbridled acceleration is the mode that overtakes us. As a result, we move forward too quickly from task to task. But a reasoned, accelerated pace is far different from a fear-induced frenetic pace.

All too often, yet another unexpected interruption occurs. It requires a return telephone call or perhaps a thoughtful and analytical response via e-mail. What do we do? How do we react to this further intrusion in our day? This over-the-edge intrusion is our real test. How well do we react? Will we avoid returning a telephone call that should be returned? Will we defer responding with the thoughtful e-mail we need to write? That's the freeze I'm talking about. Not a complete shutdown. Rather, an irrational avoidance that, with equanimity and composure, we could find the time to address.

Why do we avoid that return telephone call from the client or customer who seems to need a quick response? Is it because we don't have that little additional time to return the call? Of course not. We can always find another five minutes. Rather, it's either because we don't think we can spare the five minutes (that's our fear) or because we are afraid the call will take longer, become more involved, and require time-consuming follow-up and multiple responses (that's also our fear).

Chapter 3 | THE FEAR OF SELF-NEGOTIATION

Maybe it will, but that assumes avoidance is the best solution. Freezing in place never is. The return call can be handled in a variety of ways once we collect ourselves, realize we always have another five minutes, and face the unknown of what the client or customer has to say. What can we do?

We can:

- Return the call and say we wanted to respond immediately but are absorbed in a project that requires several more hours, after which we can discuss the matter at length, unless it cannot wait.

- We can return the call and first listen to the reason the customer or client called, analyze the time required for an appropriate response, and either realize we can get it done or share our immediate inability to do so and offer a return call later that night or the next morning.

Or

- We can force ourselves to return the call and give the conversation short-shrift, barely listening, and simply end the call as quickly as possible.

- We can call during lunch in the hope the call is not answered (hopeful avoidance).

- We can e-mail the customer or client at the end of the day, suggesting a time the next day to discuss the client's concerns.

What choice will you make? Isn't it obvious which of those responses rise up the fear ladder? But, the prison of fear is a prison without a lock—the door is always open. We just need to take a deep breath, think about the facts we know, compose ourselves, and return the call. As you make that return call, you will hear the squeaky door of your prison of fear open wide. What a great sound. You may

LAUNCHING!

experience it as that audible sigh of relief you utter (or that feeling of satisfaction) after you finish the call.

In essence, we are negotiating with ourselves. We lose when fear controls our response or nonresponse. We win when we overcome our fear. The most important negotiations in which we engage are with ourselves. How often do we ask ourselves, consciously or subconsciously, "Can I do it? Can I take on the additional assignment? Can I handle my child's school problem? Can I take care of my parent? Can I succeed?"

These are the negotiations that really count. The every day questions we ask ourselves, often without even realizing it: whether or not we can succeed, get it done. And all too often we lose the negotiation. We lose the negotiation because we are simply out negotiated by our fear.

A fear can surface in our thinking which allows us to tell ourselves, "We don't have the time" or "I can't figure it out" or "I need to speak to/get advice from Mr. or Mrs. X before I can proceed." This is fearful thinking: a thought process that freezes us in the status quo, and is riddled by the failure of inaction.

We all need to overcome the "fear factor." Just like the successful television program where contestants are asked to face their fears and overcome them, we must do the same. We need to do it if we want to grow, achieve, and succeed.

Have you watched an episode of "Fear Factor?" How did you feel when you watched contestants fail, give up part-way through, or simply not succeed? You probably admired them for trying. You may have marveled at those who succeeded, but what was your reaction to those that failed. Was it admiration? I'll bet you didn't make fun of them.

It's the same in real life. Few will mock you for trying. Ironically, those who might are probably envious you had the gumption to try, or were motivated by jealousy to hope you might fail. Should you allow those people, the naysayers, to determine your actions, to control your choices? Of course not.

Failure, in many ways, is a badge of honor. More important, it's a

Chapter 3 | THE FEAR OF SELF-NEGOTIATION

valuable learning experience. When we fail, we are given a free lesson in what we did wrong in attempting a task, whether an extra work project or a new invention. If you could ask Thomas Alva Edison, who invented the incandescent light bulb, how he felt after failing over one thousand times in his attempt to create the light bulb, what might he have said? In fact, what he did say, to paraphrase, was that he learned over one thousand ways how not to create the light bulb. In other words, each time he failed he was that much closer to discovering the correct way to reaching success.

Why do we lose so many of our self-negotiations? It's simple to understand. We allow ourselves to think with our emotions, and all too often the emotion of fear wins the negotiation. So we procrastinate and wallow in thoughts such as, "I'm not sure I can handle it," or "I don't know if I can do it."

But, successful self-negotiators trump those thoughts with thoughts of, "I'll make the time," or "I'll figure it out." And once we start to allow ourselves to think positively, our emotional response is, "I will get it done," "I can figure it out." Even more so, our rational response is a series of logical thought processes mapping out a game plan. The game plan may need to be tweaked as we move toward execution of our goal, but we've begun. And, as the saying goes (as quoted by Aristotle in his book *Politics*, although the proverb is attributed by others to the Greek oral poet, Hesiod), "Well begun is half done." Or, as I prefer, "Once begun is half done." I believe any start is a good start. Just get started! Apologies to Aristotle and Hesiod.

In a similar vein, Edgar Guest, in his perhaps not so famous poem, "It Couldn't Be Done," writes, in part:

> There are thousands to tell you it cannot be done,
> There are thousands to prophesy failure;
> There are thousands to point out to you one by one,
> The dangers that wait to assail you.
> But just buckle in with a bit of a grin,

LAUNCHING!

> Just take off your coat and go to it;
> Just start to sing as you tackle the thing
> That "cannot be done," and you'll do it.

Not only is the concept immortalized in poetry, it's also supported by the science of classical physics. It's part of Sir Isaac Newton's first law of motion. Simply put, a body in motion tends to stay in motion. It's the same with actualizing a can-do thought process by starting to execute. Sometimes the first step is as simple as putting pen to paper or, to modernize, stroking the keys of a laptop. And, all it takes to move forward to completion is just to move forward. In fact, we are the only ones who can halt the process by purposely stopping ourselves—by walking away, by giving up, by taking ourselves out of the baseball game of life and walking away from home plate back to the dugout. You are your own team self-manager. Never bench yourself!

But is it just fear that out-negotiates us so often, or is it something more? And, if it is something more, what is it and how do we overcome it? It's anxiety, stress, or tension.

All of us live with some level of these feelings, unless perhaps you are a cloistered nun or monk. In fact, stress, tension, or anxiety, like the fear factor, is our friend. We just don't realize it. These emotions can push us to greater heights; they push us to do better. Just think about Olympic athletes. How are they able to achieve personal bests or world records for the very first time at the tension-laden competition for which they have been training? It's the anxiety factor, the tension factor working for them.

Sure, it can work against them as well—but only if they allow it to translate into self-defeatism. Say, for example, when the competitor who performs just before them high jumps to a new world record. At that point, they have two options. They can allow another's success to translate into their defeat, or they can harness the energy of the other's success to propel them to achieve even greater heights—maybe not to win, but to compete admirably.

Chapter 3 | THE FEAR OF SELF-NEGOTIATION

So, the next time the boss offers you an assignment of which you are unsure—unsure if you can figure it out, unsure if you really have the time—just say yes. Take the stress test. The more times you test your stress-level muscles, the more you'll realize they won't let you down.

Yes, I said stress muscles. Think of your stress as a muscle. Aren't you surprised I have uncovered one muscle you never knew you had (there will be another muscle we'll discuss in a later chapter—the focus muscle), the stress muscle? Exercise it and you'll learn to strengthen and make it work for you. Don't let fear out negotiate you. Overcome your fear of failure. Don't join the chorus of people who chant the "If I only…" dirge. If only I:

- Went out for the team

- Took the new job

- Took the science course

- Took on the new/extra assignment

- Volunteered

- (Fill this one out yourself)

We can all win our inner negotiations. The adversary of fear is as formidable as we allow it to be, but is never as formidable as our desire to achieve, succeed, and grow. It is never as formidable as our telling ourselves, "Yes, I can."

PRACTICE POINTS

- Our biggest enemy is the "questioner" in our head—questioning our ability to go forward, take a chance, risk a failure.

- We must overcome the severity of our inner judge. We are often simply too tough on ourselves.

LAUNCHING!

- We must learn to embrace mistakes, embrace change.

- We must learn to accept that we are not perfect … that we are all far from perfect. We must learn to accept ourselves.

- When we accept ourselves and our flaws, we can more readily accept the flaws in others.

- We must remind ourselves to be an "I can" person—not an "I'll try" person.

- Success is a ladder. Some rungs are more slippery than others, but every rung is climbable with effort, focus, and perseverance.

Chapter 4

**MARKETING FOR LAWYERS
(AND OTHER PROFESSIONALS)**

LAUNCHING!

Marketing is hard for professionals. It's not what we were trained to do. Yet, we must all market ourselves, lest we be relegated to the lowest rung of the ladder—a grinder.

Professionals, it has been said, are either "finders, minders, or grinders." The first are the rainmakers, the originators. Minders are the captains and lieutenants who take responsibility for husbanding and growing new business originated by the finders, and grinders are the draftspersons and researchers.

Perhaps marketers have a special DNA that enables them to attract new clients, new business. Perhaps grinders have a special DNA that causes them to gravitate to the writing of briefs or contracts, and eschew the interpersonal skills necessary to be finders. Perhaps minders have the DNA of both finders and grinders, causing them to exhibit finder characteristics, but generally in the context of dealing with and growing existing clients, as opposed to attracting new clients.

The principles in this chapter will enhance the rainmaking ability of finders, and allow minders to allow their finder DNA to overcome their grinder DNA, at least more of the time.

Why is it so hard for lawyers to be good at marketing? It's not hard to understand. Lawyers are schooled to be smart—to learn material thoroughly and to be given clear rewards for superior performance. Let's call it the Grade-A syndrome, the desire to be the smartest in the class, the smartest in the room, to blurt out the correct answer before anyone else.

That desire works well in school and probably works well among lawyers. But it doesn't work so well with clients. Why not? Because

Chapter 4 | MARKETING FOR LAWYERS (AND OTHER PROFESSIONALS)

no one, except perhaps your parents, needs to see that you are smarter than they are. It's good to be smarter than the client, but it's not good to be demeaning, especially with clients who are in-house counsel. Why not? Because your job is to be only silently smarter than they are. Your job is to make them look smart. When it comes to marketing, you always want to make your client look good and look smart.

That's hard when you are in a conference with in-house counsel and his boss, the general counsel, questions you. Do you respond by jumping out with answers for which you are taking sole credit? Wouldn't it have been wiser to neutralize your ego and either brief in-house counsel before the meeting, or if there was no opportunity, speak in a manner that at least implies that you're presenting your ideas as a synthesis of prior conversations with in-house counsel? The point is that good marketers don't try to be the sharpest stick or brightest light in the room. They find solutions and share the credit.

Effective marketers are problem solvers. They are not sellers and not just problem finders. Problem finding and issue spotting got you a good grade on law school exams, but problem solving gets the good grade in life. Successful marketers are solvers, not sellers. Successful marketers don't just show up at a meeting with a prospective client and tout their areas of expertise and levels of capability. Rather, they engage the prospective client by asking questions. They ask questions so they can learn the needs that must be addressed and the problems that need to be solved. I wrote an entire book on the technique of mining the client's information trove to determine how you can help.

Now let's focus on how we can market ourselves to first be able to arrange to meet with a prospective new client. How does it come to pass that we are able to meet with a prospective new client? What can we do to facilitate one of the most delightful telephone calls a lawyer can receive? It starts something like this: "My friend, John Doe, and I were talking the other day. I told him I had a legal problem involving XYZ, and he suggested I call you. Can you help me?" What professional

LAUNCHING!

doesn't live for this type of call—a referral. But it wasn't a referral from a satisfied current client. It was through someone whom you know socially, and knows that you are a lawyer. That wouldn't be marketing. Good marketing creates a recommendation from a current client or a direct call or referral from a person you were prospecting. But, how can it be done? Let's take a look.

There are two obvious ways to create a noncurrent-client referral. One is by writing articles and the other is by giving speeches and presentations. Yet many lawyers both write articles and give speeches but don't generate business. Why not? Let's analyze article writing first because that is easier for most than speaking; hence, it is much more prevalent (we'll address speaking in the next chapter). Writing an article for a magazine, journal, or other media outlet has negligible positive impact. There are several reasons. Most articles are written because they address a change in the law or analyze an area of the law. But shouldn't an article be written to address a need and be directed to those who have the need? Good marketing techniques would suggest so, but articles are written for other reasons too. They can be an opportunistic way to publish, and many consider them to be resume builders. But are they? And if they are resume builders, how many prospective clients read that carefully, that far into a resume? Usually, the "selected published works" part of a resume is at the end and is unlikely to be focused heavily on.

Good marketers understand most articles are not read, except when the need arises. In other words, an article crossing a recipient's desk, either in a magazine or journal, or via direct mail, will be either discarded, or saved so the reader may look at it when the need arises. Since effective marketers value their time, they try to write articles for specific audiences who are more likely to have a current reason to read the article. They know that at least 95 percent of the article's potential readers will not read it and the few percent—if that much—who save it may never look at it anyway, even when the need arises. Why not? They filed the article away and then forgot about it.

Chapter 4 | MARKETING FOR LAWYERS
(AND OTHER PROFESSIONALS)

Ah, timing is everything.

What do effective marketers do to heighten the chance that they will write for the most receptive audience? It's easy. They analyze who the potential clients are, and write in publications most likely to be read by that population. It's simple. If a lawyer has a specialty that lends itself to referral work, the likely audience is other lawyers practicing in the same jurisdiction. For example, a specialist in appellate and Supreme Court work (assuming those courts are the highest and second-highest courts in the particular jurisdiction) would consider his target market to be other lawyers—trial lawyers in particular, on the assumption that lower-court cases, from which the appeals process emanates, are being handled by attorneys practicing in the same jurisdiction. However, in-state referrals are few and far between, unless you practice in a specialty that truly lends itself to referrals. Why? Simply because the competition loathes sending out a case if they can handle it. Litigators are omnipresent in the legal profession. Hence, normal litigation is not a fertile referral source. On the other hand, a specialty such as product liability is.

But why limit yourself to in-state referrals? Referrals from out-of-state practitioners could be a much broader source of business. Hence, why not write for regional or national publications as well, or even spend the majority of your time writing for such publications, particularly when the same article can also be used for your home state periodicals? Better yet, why not write for the ultimate end user, the client? How do effective marketers reach the end-user client? It's not so simple. It requires investigation and research. For example, the ultimate end user for an article on, say, corporate taxation, is likely to be someone in the finance or tax department of a corporation. But what does such a person, a business person, read? How does the effective marketer find out?

For virtually every area of the law and every analog area of business, there is probably a conference and a trade magazine dealing with one or

29

LAUNCHING!

more legal or business sectors to which the conference and the magazine cater. It just requires finding out the name of the conference and the names of the magazines. Just as there are skiing industry magazines, there are magazines and journals and maybe even conferences that are in the business of catering and selling to industries in which you practice. Magazines are businesses, and their editors are always looking for good articles from reliable authors who meet word count and time deadlines, just as conference organizers seek dynamic speakers who can present effective, value-added material.

So, how does an effective marketer start the investigative process? The Internet has greatly simplified the search. Once the conference catering to an industry in which you practice is discovered, the organizing group is determined, and the associated magazine or journal is uncovered, the real work begins. Effective marketers know that their job is to make the job of the conference organizer and magazine editor as easy as possible. Since effective marketers know it can take several years to break into a conference-speaking role, they create a multi-year plan to achieve their objective. They first attend the conference to determine if the attendees reflect their target market. They analyze the nature of the speakers/panels and study the content presented. Is the conference slanted toward a particular sector of the industry, a specific legal or business aspect, or is it broader than you expected? Are the attendees high enough in the corporate hierarchy to influence hiring decisions, or are they corporate in-house grinders?

Let's assume the marketer analyzes the attendees and determines an eventual speaking role at the conference could be an effective marketing tool for new business. Since he knows, given the politics of the conference, that it may take several years to earn a speaking role, what can he do now? He can seek to write in the sponsoring organization's publication. He obtains the last several years of publications of the organization's magazine. Since the conference is primarily for businesspersons and clients, he reads the publications to determine if lawyers are ever authors and, if so, if the same authors recur with little change. Let's assume the publication contains one or two articles written by lawyers in every edition. What does the effective marketer do next? The effective marketer studies each article to understand the nature of the topics addressed, the level of the article, and whether or not the word count of the articles is similar.

By studying the nature of the topics, he can determine subtopic gaps that he can fill. By analyzing the level of the article, he can determine if the editor and the reader seek a layman's approach or a law review approach, or something in the middle. He can immediately see if footnotes are used. Last, by simply counting the words, he can determine if a particular length is sought or if word count is flexible. Sounds stupid? It's not. Why not?

The best articles ever written won't get published if they don't fit the format. Remember, for the editor, it's business. It's content, format, timeliness, topicality, and, most important, word count. If the article doesn't fit, it won't be published.

So, what's the next step for the effective marketer? After determining a suitable article topic, writing it, and falling within the word count range, he can send it to the editor. But will that likely be effective? Probably not, because the editor:

- Does not know you

- Receives an overwhelming amount of submissions

- Has authors she already uses and trusts, who know what she needs and expects

- Does not know you

- Does not know you

So what can a good marketer do to become a new contributor in the XYZ business association quarterly magazine? The marketer has found the problem. It was easy. The editor needs two pieces of good,

LAUNCHING!

legal-oriented content per publication. She needs new and interesting topics all the time, and she needs the article to run, say, between 1,700 and 2,000 words. The effective marketer has the solution. How might he present the solution to the editor or one of her assistants? Let's find out.

Rather than sending an email, he picks up the telephone (remember that invention by Alexander Graham Bell) and continues to call until he reaches a member of the editorial staff. Since he joined the trade association, he introduces himself as a member and quickly explains how he has not seen an article on XYZ topic and that he is in the process of putting the finishing touches on one which is on topic (he already wrote it). He then asks if she is interested and also asks the length necessary for publication (he already knew the required length - he did his homework). If she likes the topic and has an interest in reading and considering such an article for publication, he then tells her the length of his piece. The next step should be delivery of the article and follow-up. She still may not read it, because she has a backlog of articles to carry her for the next four quarterly editions, so she won't get to it for nine months or more. That spells, "Maybe never." Hence, follow-up is critical.

Effective marketers know that presentation, in and of itself, is not nearly enough. Presentation must come at a critical juncture in time. The editor needs to be conscious of the availability and readiness of the article when she is seeking to lay out material for the next publication or set of publications.

Is it any different, in any context, for any professional? What's the point of a cardiac surgeon selling himself when a cardiac situation does not exist, or a trial lawyer selling himself when the client is currently litigation-free? And what's the assurance that there will not be an intervening event when the patient needs a cardiac surgeon? For example, in the surgery context, a family member makes the selection, or in the legal context, a business peer recommends his litigation attorney.

Timing is often everything, and that is an element that no one can effectively control. So, if you didn't get published in a reasonable period of time, try again.

Remember the platinum rule. If at first you don't succeed, try, try, try, try ... try, try, try ... try, try, try ... then try again.

PRACTICE POINTS

- Speaking is not enough.

- Writing articles is not enough.

- Speak and write. But that's not enough.

- Obtain high quality reprints of your article and send them, via snail mail, with a cover letter, to every appropriate contact in your database.

- Business development requires many "touches." Speak, write, mail ... follow-up, if appropriate, with a telephone call.

Chapter 5
ORGANIZATIONAL MARKETING

LAUNCHING!

In the last chapter we touched upon speaking for organizations. There are fundamentally two tracks for lawyers—bar associations and trade associations (it's a similar dual track for other professions as well). The altruistic and the "resume builders" focus on bar associations. The marketers seeking new business focus on trade associations. It's easy to understand why.

Bar association presentations attract few outside lawyers. They are meant to provide legal education credits for various skill levels in almost all of the specializations comprising the practice of law. It's a good thing to do. I do it. But it doesn't get you clients, because potential clients are seldom in attendance.

Clients, whether in-house counsel or businesspersons, tend to associate with their own kind at trade associations. Outside lawyers are also in attendance, if permitted, but most outside lawyers do not attend trade association conferences. Why not? Perhaps it is because there are so few other outside lawyers (actually a great reason to attend), or because the topics are just too business-oriented. The latter is an even better reason to attend. Why? Because clients want to deal with lawyers who already understand their business.

Clients do not want to pay for a lawyer to go to school "on their dime." In fact, the next time you have a chance to work for a new client in a business or industry of which you have little knowledge, ask the client to allow you to meet with him, inspect his business operations, and get to better understand both, all on your dime. No charge. That's right. No charge! You may be pleasantly surprised at the result. On the other hand, if you are fearful you will not be hired because of

Chapter 5 | ORGANIZATIONAL MARKETING

your lack of knowledge of the prospective client's business or industry, research, study, and learn about it in advance of the meeting. There is so much information readily available, especially if the prospect works for a public company. But even if the prospect's company is private, you can still learn a great deal from publically available information. Just study a comparable publicly traded company in the same business or same industry.

You say it's too much to do for a prospect; you'll wait until you are hired. Now, what is the thinking behind that delayed approach? Let's see. Your ego is telling you that you are too busy and perhaps too important. Maybe you're just lazy. Perhaps you just cannot find the time. Of course you have the time! That's what nights and weekends are for—even vacations. So you're not interested in curling up with some annual reports of the company and some industry analysis reports, all of which are readily obtainable on the Internet either on your target company or a publicly traded analog. Hmmm. Sounds like a grinder to me—not a minder and certainly not a finder. It's your choice.

Let's return to trade associations and their conferences and meetings. The attendees are the oil wells. But how do we find them and then drill down to extract the oil? Just like oil wells, all deposits are not equal. In fact, many, if not most, will be dry holes. Some will have small, uneconomic deposits, and others will simply be unreachable. The key is to focus your time and attention in order to identify and drill the profitable ones.

How do we accomplish our investigation? What are the techniques? They are simple. Just as geologists study an area to determine likely profitable deposits, we must do the same. Our exploration, however, does not require geospatial analysis and expensive test wells. Lawyers and other professionals test through introduction and conversation. So what should you do at any conference, bar meeting, or social gathering? Avoid your legal peers. Stick your hand out and introduce yourself to strangers. No one said it's easy or that it necessarily comes naturally. But that's what effective marketers do, that's what finders

LAUNCHING!

do. They seek to make introductions. They don't seek to give out their business cards. They seek to collect business cards. They know the path to "finding" is a function of the number of business cards they receive. Why? Because giving a business card is passive. Who knows if it will be thrown away when the prospect returns to his office, or even sooner, when he goes back to his hotel room? On the other hand, when a prospect hands you his business card it suggests that he is inviting you to communicate with him. Even if you are not sure of his intention, assume the positive.

But what if you are a stranger at a conference? Everyone seems to know each other and act as if they know what they are doing and where they are going. What should you do?

- Go to every presentation. When there are concurrent presentations, select carefully. Presentations on particular topics may recur infrequently. Don't forego opportunities.

- At each presentation, do not sit in the back looking as if you are ready to sneak out early.

- Be engaged. Read all presentation materials before the presentation so you are a prepared and informed listener, so that the time you are spending as a member of the audience is as productive as possible.

- Do not sit at the end of a row. Arrive at the presentation early (because early is the new on-time), and sit between two strangers. In the down time before the presentation, introduce yourself. Ask them the opening pleasantry questions about themselves. Let them talk! This is a fact-gathering mission. That's right—conferences are work!

- Be on the look out for a short question-and-answer period near the end. This end-of-presentation opportunity, when it presents itself, will give you the chance to shine. How? Because you

Chapter 5 | ORGANIZATIONAL MARKETING

prepared, and you were hoping there would be sufficient time for a Q & A so you could ask a crisp and incisive question. Why? Because great questions show your mettle. As a mentor once said to me, "Anyone can look up the answers. Success is a function of asking the right questions."

- Seek out the program planners and the association staff. Ask them how you can become more involved. Tell them you like the association, like the conference, and are volunteering for any job—that's right, any job.

- As a rule, volunteers rise to the top in associations, even when there are political headwinds. Let's face it, you're the new kid on the block, so give it time. Be solicitous without being pushy.

- Take any role you can get (it may take a year or two to find the right door).

- If you are offered a speaking role, say as a roundtable leader, prepare as if you were the keynote speaker. You'll be noticed. It works. It worked for me.

- Most important, give all of your techniques and secrets away. Never hold back. When you give it away, the universe will always repay you in manifold ways, although exactly how it repays you may not be immediately obvious. Trust me. It works.

- When you are invited to be a panelist, don't just be a lawyer. Be a business lawyer. Make it practical. Make it value enhancing. Make sure you leave the audience with valuable take-aways.

LAUNCHING!

- Avoid anecdotes, war stories, and fluffy opinions. Do not assume the audience will enjoy your stories. Do not assume that you are Jay Leno and the audience seeks to be entertained. Always assume everyone in the audience considers their time to be valuable, the cost of the conference is dear, and that they are attending solely to be educated and learn. Speak like a newscaster.

- Offer tips, facts, and new ideas.

So, it's three years later and you've gotten zero business from attending these meetings. But you've earned the opportunity to chair a panel. Now you're getting to pay dirt. Why? Because the treasure is the relationships you make, and the best relationships often come from the preparation with your panelists over the months preceding the presentation. This is your chance to let your panelists shine and, at the same time, exhibit your knowledge of the topic on which the panel is speaking, your leadership, and your ability to navigate the group from scratch to a successful conclusion.

Assume the presentation goes well. Of course it did. You led a well-prepared group. So, not surprisingly, many in the audience come up to talk to each of you at the end of the presentation. That's great, but they are not your target clients. Your target clients are your panelists, whether you solicited them or the organization leader or conference chair selected them for you. Don't run to the attendees. The oil is your co-panelists. They now know you—they've worked with you and conducted a successful presentation with you. Drill those wells.

So what's next? It's the bad part! Once you leave the speaker's stage and melt into the crowd, you once again feel like you are anonymous. It's the come-down from the adrenaline rush of speaking. It's normal, so face it, disregard it, and overcome it. You're exhilarated and a bit drained at the same time. So what do you do? Follow the rules and techniques above. Dust yourself off and start all over again. There are more wells to drill, and finders keep at it.

Chapter 5 | ORGANIZATIONAL MARKETING

That's "conference-ology 202." You're way past the basics at this stage.

PRACTICE POINTS

- The platinum rule for finders is "try, try, try, try, try, try, try, try, try, try, try, try … then, try again!

- Being a panelist is a great speaking opportunity, and a good marketing opportunity.

- Chairing a panel is a great marketing opportunity.

Chapter 6

**MARKETING
(TIMELINESS AND COMMUNICATION)**

LAUNCHING!

A good performance requires two non-substantive elements: timeliness and communication. Even when we complete a project on time, it may not be enough. Why not? Let's take a typical example.

We are given an assignment from our superior or our client together with a deadline of two weeks. It's a tough assignment requiring research and a significant amount of drafting. We bury ourselves in the project virtually to the exclusion of almost all else (that's a failure; we'll discuss that later). We work continuously and we present the document—say, a contract or a brief—on the scheduled day to our superior or our boss. Is that the A?

What did we fail to do? First and perhaps foremost, in today's service-oriented practice of law (actually, any service business ... actually any business!), early is the new on time. Let's examine why. Assume you were expecting a car service to pick you up and take you to the airport to catch a flight to a destination served by only one flight per day. The pickup is arranged for 8:15 a.m. In fact, the driver arrives at 8:15 a.m.—on time. How did you feel in the fifteen or twenty minutes prior to his on-time arrival? You probably felt anxious, wondering if he would arrive on time. As the clock approached 8:15 a.m., did the seconds seem like minutes as your anxiety level continued to rise?

Is it any different in any context? Unless the deadline is unimportant, stress will always increase as a function of the unknown. What should the driver—you—have done?

- Take into account all possible contingencies: traffic, construction, weather, etc.

Chapter 6 | MARKETING (TIMELINESS AND COMMUNICATION)

- Call in advance to furnish an update: "I'm ten minutes away."

- Always plan to beat a deadline—that way you create a hopefully unnecessary contingency cushion. If you don't need it, even better. You beat the deadline.

Oh, but you say you're too busy to worry about blowing deadlines. In fact, you might even think a slight delay is okay. Why? Because you're doing important, hard, brain-challenging work? That's your ego talking. Your ego is not in a service business, but you are.

So, you're surprised when you get the assignment done, but there is no repeat business. Why? Because you are in a service business. You did a great job on the brain part of practicing law but you actually failed the service part. If you created anxiety for your boss or your client, if your lack of communication caused follow-up and check-in calls from your boss or your client, you failed the service part. Harsh? No. It's reality. Your ego can tell you that you did a great job, or wrote a great brief, or drafted a terrific document, but always remember that your ego is your enemy. It tries to convince you how important you are, what a terrific draftsperson you are, which may be true. But you must remember that service is your most important product. Just ask General Electric. That was its advertising slogan.

Let's see the other hidden failures you committed. Remember how hard you worked to complete the brief or document? Your ego felt as if you were working day and night. In fact, you were so busy with the project that you worked on it without regard to your other responsibilities. Your ego told you that was okay. Remember?

Well, it wasn't okay. Let's see what you failed to do. Did any of the following happen? Were you asked by a superior or another client to "look at something for him" and let him know? Rather than do so and determine if you could fit the project in, did you say you were just too busy? Did you receive any telephone calls from clients asking for a return telephone call that you simply refused to allow yourself to make for one or more days? Wait, that's not service. Did you delay responding

LAUNCHING!

for one or more hours? Why? Were you afraid the conversation would take too long? That it would require follow-up and pull you away from your assigned project? Did you simply ignore the call? For how long—more than six hours, beyond the day you received it, or longer? What "service grade" does that deserve? Your ego will give you at least a C, but it's a D or an F in the real world.

What's happened? Years ago delay was not only permitted from lawyers, it was almost expected and more often than not accepted. What's changed? Well, just about everything. Blame the Internet. Blame e-mails, Twitter, you name it. Response time has telescoped, and shrunk. But common courtesy and manners have not changed and will never change. Why not? Because human nature remains a constant. The amalgam of emotions that constitutes human nature is woven into the fabric of our species.

So, how should we handle longer projects which will inevitably be interspersed with interruption?

- Provide periodic updates; make the time and take the time to do so. The boss or client does not know what you are doing, how far you have progressed, or whether or not you'll meet the deadline.

- Don't be afraid of being interrupted. Perhaps the client only needs five minutes of your time. What if it's a new piece of business? What if they are simply checking in for a status update? By the way, that would be a yellow flag—the client is nervous. Your ego tells you he shouldn't be nervous. He should know you are diligent and will timely complete the matter. Hmmm. Think of how you felt while waiting at the front door for your 8:15 a.m. pickup before receiving a telephone call from the driver. When do you begin to become anxious? At 8:10 a.m., or earlier perhaps at 8:00 a.m., 7:45 a.m., 7:30 a.m.?

Remember, a response (to anything) becomes less effective as a function of the length of time in which it takes to respond. Provide updates. Your ego may not want to but your humility quotient will thank you. Remember, fear is our enemy. Don't be afraid to respond to what you fear may be a return call that will distract you or cause you to have to take a slight detour on your way to the finish line. Allow yourself to be interrupted—don't listen to your ego. Worse, don't allow your fears to freeze you into a delayed response or none at all. You can do it all. Just allow yourself to flex your elevated anxiety muscles. With a little practice, and "a deep breath and a step back," all will become clear and you will service each client effectively.

PRACTICE POINTS

- A job well done is only well done if the recipient thinks so.

- Providing updates nourishes our humility.

- There's always a little extra time to answer the call, return the e-mail, exercise our grace.

- Stress and anxiety are just a state of mind.

- Belief in ourselves and belief in our ability to get it all done is a better state of mind.

Chapter 7
THE ZEN OF COLONY

LAUNCHING!

Colonization has become a dirty word—we tend to think of formerly oppressed peoples in Africa and the Americas. Of course, colonization also conjures up excitement, adventure, and optimism as we let our imaginations consider exploration of the moon and beyond.

But that's not the type of colony I am referring to. I am thinking of the mighty ant, weak and at peril when alone, yet collectively a strong and fearsome predator as part of a colony.

New research, aided by advanced photography, has demonstrated how a colony of ants unifies all the thoughts (reactions) of each member ant. Each ant acts as a cell in a larger living organism. They seem to "combine" both mentally and physically. When they move, apart from the scouts, they often seem to move as a single lump of coordinated living matter. What a sight! Just watch the Discovery or Science channels and notice how any other living creature that is mobile just knows to get out of their way—no matter how large, how strong, and how hungry.

When a million tiny minds act as one and virtually combine into a single unified organism, each becomes larger, stronger, and immeasurably more effective than when acting independently of the others. Yes, those brave scouts, acting as if independent of the colony but in concert with other brave scouts, remain vulnerable and far from fearsome. Yet, they, too, act in a unified way with the colony to risk their lives as they probe the unknown for either a new home or new food source for the colony.

Of course, this book is not about myrmecology (that's the official name for the study of ants—I Googled it) and certainly not about entomology (that's the study of bugs). So let's get to the point. How does it occur that millions of ant minds think, live, and work as one, thereby increasing the likelihood of the success and continuation of the colony? Even more, how is it that they seem to maintain that unification of purpose all the time? And, if it works so well for ants, why do we humans seem to be moving in the opposite direction, towards isolation? I will say more about that later on.

Don't all great leaders, just like the ant queen, seek to do the same for their colony and its members—to foster unification? If the goal of every leader is to increase the health of the entity, and ensure its prosperity and growth, how can a leader be as effective as the ant queen?

Maybe the queen actually has it too easy. Why? Because the colony is almost always potentially threatened with its destruction—which is certainly a highly unifying motivator. But, that's seldom the case for companies or even countries. Or is it?

Of course it is—it's just that threats are seldom as obvious as they are to Lilliputian ants. So, if threats are often unseen, what defense (or is it also an offense?) must the effective leader employ to ensure the survival, success, and growth of the organization?

It's the constant strengthening of the community of the organization. Of course, any individual should be helped to grow, but a company of independent growers, (let's call them "silos"), is less likely to coalesce during the hard times. It's less likely—actually unlikely—that the silos will bond when bonding is required—when the company, or any entity, is under economic attack. It's just harder to bond, because the organization hasn't really learned how.

Forming relationships and bonds takes work. Hard work! It's hard work because self-starting, hard-charging employees all too often see the effort as a distraction. Effective leaders know this. Effective leaders know they must affirmatively push camaraderie and affirmatively shut down back-biting, petty jealousy, and negative comments about others. Effective leaders must constantly seek to unify. They must affirmatively

LAUNCHING!

shut down negativity. Passivity won't do.

Effective leaders know it's just not enough to "let it pass." They must proactively neutralize the negativity of jealousy, independence to a fault, and unfettered internal competition. They must always seek to soften these negatives, even eradicate them. Competition is healthy, but leaders must foster competition that incentivizes employees to grow and excel and avoid creating competition that causes employees to subvert and undermine others. How else can community ever take hold and develop?

Let's consider two ants, Adam Ant (not the rocker) and George Ant (Adam's cousin), and their Queen, Charlotte (not the German monarch for whom a city in North Carolina was named). Do you think Adam Ant ever goes to his queen to complain that George Ant is not pulling his weight? That George Ant was slacking on the last mission? Or, do you think Adam Ant and his buddies just take it upon themselves to push George forward (both physically and chemically) to get the job done? No doubt it is the latter. Why? Because of their sense of community—its positive force. The healthy interconnections it breeds makes each constituent want to do the right thing—to take actions supporting or furthering the common good. Ant colonies are millions of ants being pushed to act as a unit by the invisible binding and unifying force of the colony. It certainly appears that way whenever the colony is on the march.

Community is much more than an abstract concept. It's a strength builder, a health builder and more. Community is often a survival technique, especially in the animal world. How else could emperor penguins otherwise survive the extreme cold of the Antarctic? By literally huddling together, they survive the winter. They maintain their proximity so that the penguins on the outside shield the others from the extreme cold, while all enjoy the heat preservation of the huddle. Of course, the penguins continuously shift the huddle so all enjoy the warm interiors, and all participate in the exterior shield. In fact, community can grow cities and enhance the health of its citizenry or it can topple governments. Let's see how.

In a speech delivered at a shopping center convention in Las Vegas, the famous contemporary author Malcolm Gladwell made several fascinating observations, two of which continue to resonate within me.

The first was about the inhabitants of a little medieval foothill town in Roseto Valfortore, Italy. Over time, virtually the entire town migrated to the same place in Pennsylvania. It thrived as it grew and developed during the 1950s. Ironically, during this decade, which is considered by some to have been the "heart-attack decade" for men then in their fifties, the heart attack rate of the community's new home was well below the-then national average for that demographic. Medical experts struggled to understand why. Neither diet, nor lifestyle, nor "gene pool" studies provided an answer. Eventually, it was concluded that it was the nature of the community. It was close-knit with an extraordinarily high level of civic and religious community participation. According to Mr. Gladwell, the environment of the community really matters, as set forth in the foreword to his book, *Outliers*, where he discusses the work and findings of Stewart Wolf, a physician, and John Bruhn, a sociologist.

Let's consider the second of Mr. Gladwell's observations, about one of the most important participants, Egypt, in the "Arab Spring." After several weeks of protests and strikes in Tahir Square, President Mubarak resigned. But how did the populace reach the point of overthrowing their dictator in a society of secret police, oppression, and the rule of fear? We all know the Internet allowed atrocities to go viral, and enabled the citizenry to obtain the news and communicate with each other. The news media described the overthrow as a triumph of social media. But, according to Mr. Gladwell, it wasn't the media, and it wasn't the Internet that was the real cause of the overthrow. What then brought a fearful populace out of their homes to risk beatings and dreaded jail? According to Mr. Gladwell, the overthrow became actualized when the pipes of communication were shut down. Mr. Gladwell speculates that the populace left their homes and the safety of the Internet when President Mubarak ordered the Internet shut down. As a result, having

LAUNCHING!

lost the sense of community they had from their interconnection on the Internet, the population migrated out of their homes to their physical "places of community." They went to their mosques and their age-old community park, Tahir Square. In essence, the government unintentionally turned each ant, formerly using its own Internet silo, from a virtual community into a physical community of ants. They needed to continue to communicate after the Internet was shut down so they did it the old fashioned way, even at the risk of bodily injury. They met in the places of community engrained in their beings, engrained in their culture, developed over the lifetime of their civilization. Hence, the community got the "W" (the win) and the despot got the "L" (the loss).

Yet, anti-community-ism is developing as a function of the rise of the virtual community, the rise of the social machine. It's all around us. Anti-community-ism has an insidious negative impact on all families—personal, corporate, or sovereign. Effective leaders see this development as a constant low-temperature, low-grade infection seeking to expand itself to all levels of the family—personal, corporate, and country. Perhaps it's not an infection. Perhaps it's just information-socialization overload—perhaps a kind of (instantaneous) solution pollution.

Effective leaders know that community and connection do not occur naturally in human nature. Our digital age beckons us with the ease of immediate access to information and knowledge. It gives us access to a virtual community of knowledge and people and virtual participation (but not real communication in real time with real-time participants). In return for these benefits, we become increasingly physically alone. Yet, we don't feel alone. We are communicating, but we're not physically interacting. Are we being lulled into a world of virtual interaction? Imagine the life span of a colony of ants if they could communicate long distance, via their antennae, thereby permitting greater distance between and among them. I think we can speculate that their life span would be materially shortened.

Effective leaders understand this. They understand the decline in

Chapter 7 | THE ZEN OF COLONY

family intimacy and workplace intimacy. According to recent studies the average size of our intimate circles has decreased from approximately three individuals to approximately two. In other words, the number of those with whom we would share our most private thoughts has shrunk dramatically. Parents spend less time with their children, even less with their teenagers, and most of us spend less time with our friends and colleagues. Doesn't seem like much, but it's a one-third drop in our intimacy index. (I would speculate that the citizenry of Roseto Valfortore experienced an increase in the intimacy index during the fifties.)

To foster community, effective leaders must find common goals among employees. Often, they need to create new goals or adjust current goals. Effective leaders are always on the lookout for common goals. They are always on the lookout for creeping isolationism. They seek out and engage those who seek to withdraw into their own private world, whether or not virtual. They seek to knit the bonds of community. Attacks on community are almost always insidious; they come in so many forms:

- Carping

- Avoidance

- Disinterest, and

- Reduced participation

But, effective leaders overcome isolationism by creating a vibrant core. The best leaders create multiple cores. Effective leaders understand that leadership is all about managing the managers! It's almost like planets around a sun. Having more planets increases the likelihood that their gravitational pull will draw other objects to the sun. Effective leaders understand celestial physics. By creating more managers and enhancing their status, authority, and respect, effective leaders are applying the glue necessary to further knit the community. Fearful leaders fear the process of creating managers, at least managers

LAUNCHING!

with real authority. Effective leaders know better. Their captains and lieutenants are the true building blocks of community—they are essential.

Effective leaders understand, as does Mr. Gladwell, that community brings a greater sense of being to people's lives. The spirit of any family comes alive. People feel rejuvenated—more a part of something, and more likely to stay connected and work to help each other. Why? Community creates a sense of purpose, thereby enhancing the spirit of the whole and somehow reinforcing the greater goal—the greater good. The human spirit is uplifted by working for a purpose greater than the individual.

But leaders know it's not that simple. In small towns like Roseto Valfortore, community is centered around the church. But families and companies are not churches, unless everyone is praying to Mammon, the god of money.

So what do effective leaders need to do to create community? Social events are good for lots of obvious reasons, but the communal glue cannot be solely composed of bread, wine, and good times. There must be more—much more. Of course, there must be a common purpose—a purpose comprising spirit, ethics, and a mutual respect, as well as an unflinching adherence to the principles of truth and honesty.

Everyone cannot like everyone else. Insecurity and jealousy foment isolation. Not everyone can perform as well as others. Effective leaders get it. They understand that it's not a competition between family members or employees except in the rarest of circumstances. They understand that each employee is a work in progress. Each must improve to the best of his ability and then push himself to yet a higher level through the supportive power of community.

Anti-community-ism is all around us. It's our fears, our jealousies, the Internet, our bad luck—everything that sours us. Leaders know it. Effective leaders work to overcome the seduction of self-pity. They not only identify and communicate goals, they seek to build bridges for all to reach those goals. They communalize the success of the group so everyone succeeds by virtue of anyone's success. Tough to do? Not really.

It starts with creating and enhancing an *esprit de corps*, fostering a feeling that one person's or one team's success is the community's success, the organization's success. It's as simple as translating the positive impact of a gold-medal Olympian returning home from her victory at the Olympiad into a victory for her hometown by allowing the town to become a part of her success via parades and the like. Although it starts with personal pride, it quickly morphs into the wonderful feelings of sharing and communal ownership.

Success can also be made more tangible. In the corporate-business context, it can be monetized, for example, by a two-tiered bonus pool, which is a concept used effectively by many companies. The first tier is an employee-based bonus for individual performance, and the second tier is an organization-wide bonus for total organizational performance regardless of any individual's efforts, and regardless of the source of the profits.

You don't need to feel as vulnerable as an ant or be as cold as an emperor penguin to use community effectively for the growth of all of its members.

PRACTICE POINTS

- Avoid isolation.

- Don't rely on the Internet for communication. It's virtual—and no matter how fast it becomes, it still lacks true interpersonal real-time interchange.

- Stay more in real time. Stop hitting the keys. Use the telephone. Better yet, meet in person.

- There is strength in numbers—sometimes the strongest bonds are unseen.

Chapter 8
THE NEGOTIATION OF MOTIVATION

LAUNCHING!

The best financial advisors are excellent at handling a client's assets. Similarly, the best trial lawyers are superior litigators and adept at working with judges and juries, just as the best doctors are proficient at diagnosis and excellent at performing their specialty procedures. A hallmark of most successful people is their ability to excel at their chosen profession and deal effectively with their clients and customers.

So why is it that so often individuals such as these allow themselves to diffuse their energy by either being thrust into, or actively seeking, positions of management? Why do people think that their ability to sell a product, advise a client, try a case, or perform a medical procedure, qualifies them to be managers, or even leaders?

For those who break out of the solo mode and work with a team, the basis for greater management, even leadership, is at least partially formed. For those who operate as a successful single-piston engine, it would be more prudent to be disinclined or even averse to management and leadership. Yet, many of us seek greater responsibility. So often it is those not yet trained in the skills of management and leadership who nevertheless seek to assume, to one degree or another, such positions.

Let's see what leaders can do to help develop the skills necessary for their future lieutenants and captains and eventual successor. How can leaders instill managerial skills? How do leaders motivate others to be more effective managers? It's by teaching them to make decisions and, whenever possible and appropriate to the nature of the issue, to make them quickly. It's okay to evaluate—it's not okay to procrastinate.

Decision making for many is hard. The fear of making mistakes or

Chapter 8 | THE NEGOTIATION OF MOTIVATION

the fear of failure lurks behind not only every poor decision but, much worse, behind every less-than-optimal decision. But does it? And if it does, what must leaders instill in their subordinates to overcome those fears?

Imagine what would happen in your local supermarket if the store manager was unable to make quick decisions. What decision must be made when an employee calls in sick? What if the employee is late, never called in, and was unreachable by telephone, thus leaving the store manager to decide whether or not to replace him that day?

What if a delivery truck was late with critical foodstuffs for the shelves? What if adverse weather approaches much faster than the forecasters predicted? The best store managers take quick and decisive action, and effective leaders seek those types of individuals for the position.

If the only constant in business is change and if the pace of change continuously accelerates, then the best course of action is to promote and train those who exhibit an ability to respond decisively to ever-changing circumstances on a fairly rapid basis.

Yet, how often do leaders sabotage the very trait they seek? While it's easy for a leader to tell a subordinate he did okay and should work to do better, it's not easy to hide the look of disappointment, perhaps even scorn, which can surface for a nanosecond before the leader catches himself. The problem is that nanosecond of unmasked disappointment can appear to the other as a judgment of utter failure, a nanosecond that can feel like hours in the eyes of the beholder, regardless of the reassuring words that follow.

How can leaders avoid that chilling look? By avoiding face-to-face surprise? Yes, but not by avoiding the face-to-face meeting. If a leader needs an update and doesn't know what the news will be, why not get some advance intelligence first. In the store manager context, perhaps the leader first asked about the status from the district manager. Or, if the report must be direct, perhaps start via telephone, thereby getting some sense of the news prior to meeting in person. Then, at the in-person

LAUNCHING!

meeting, the leader can review the decision-tree matrix employed by the subordinate if the situation warrants. And when nevertheless surprised in a face-to-face meeting, he will ingest the information with equanimity, and rather than a snap response—start with, "That's interesting news, tell me more so I can better understand the situation." Effective leaders are "never act surprised" leaders. Effective leaders are "tell me more" leaders.

At the in-person meeting, which may be just a two-minute conversation, the leader must then work to instill the confidence that enables decisions to be made quickly and decisively. It is at that meeting that the leader instills the concept that decision making requires a decision to effect success, even when that decision requires later adjustment. Effective leaders must instill the concept that decision making is a success if it is the best decision that can be made with the facts then known and it is decisive and clear.

A murky, unclear, and indecisive decision is as bad as no decision at all—maybe worse. Why? Because a decision that is indecisive or unclear begets multiple potential courses of action. Imagine if a sergeant told his men they should "take one of those hills over there" as opposed to "take the first hill, the hill directly in front of you with the rocky cliff on one side."

It's the same in business. Clear decisions are almost always the best decisions and always good decisions, unless they are made without facts that are readily available or they are made based on emotion. Decisions made without having all the available facts are decisions made by the unprepared and therefore likely misinformed. Decisions made based on emotion are decisions that should be postponed until the emotions can be neutralized (and only the facts remain). Remember, emotions are our internal gusts of wind. When we emotionalize, we stir up the facts we know like leaves on a tree. They shake and shimmy and become blurred until our emotions are neutralized and our internal gusts of wind die down. Only in the ensuing calm can we see the facts clearly.

Ah, but you said quick, effective decision making is the goal. It is,

Chapter 8 | THE NEGOTIATION OF MOTIVATION

unless it's tainted with emotion. Ironically, the exception to obtaining all the then-available information all too often becomes the rule. Why? Because of the speed of change, emergency decisions must often be made even without the opportunity to obtain all of the otherwise readily available information. Hence, effective leaders teach others to anticipate. By instilling anticipation—the concept of "what if" analysis—employees become more comfortable with on-the-spot decision making. More important, they begin to understand, and to digest, the concept that a clear decision under the circumstances is usually a good one.

So how do leaders handle the employee who seems to seek preapproval for many decisions, regardless of importance? There are several negotiating techniques.

The first method is the passive-effective approach, entailing temporary delay. Allow the request for a decision to go temporarily unanswered. Perhaps purposely defer the response to an e-mail or a telephone call. We all know most decisions can be made by the subordinate. Time often resolves the issue, either because a good decision becomes self-evident or, left to his own devices, the employee makes (or is forced to make) the decision.

The second method is the "quasi-active-effective" approach. Instead of allowing the exigencies of the moment to cause the leader to quietly furnish the decision or bark the decision, the leader takes the few extra leadership moments and creates a social dialectic by asking a series of questions along the theme of "What would you do?" or "Why would you do it?" and, "How do you think it will play out?"

But the employee still remains frozen, refuses to take the responsibility, and continues to press for direction. Why? Almost every subordinate believes the boss will make the better decision and most subordinates are simply insecure and afraid to be wrong. Of course, some will make decisions on their own even when the better alternative was to seek advice. The employee in the first scenario must be allowed to make the decision. He must be taught that a poor decision,

LAUNCHING!

by itself, is not failure. It's simply a less than optimal decision. That employee must learn to "pull the trigger." The employee in the second scenario needs to adjust his thought process to understand when to seek advice by realizing it is not a badge of weakness, but can be a sign of strength. A poor decision is only a poor decision—not failure. Failure is either a poor decision left unadjusted or a poor decision compounded by yet another (too quickly made and/or emotionally charged) poor decision.

Effective leaders always perform post-decision analysis. They negotiate with their subordinates to teach the elements and value of decision making, the ability to understand when a ten-minute or one-hour or one-week delay is appropriate in order to obtain additional facts – and when an immediate decision must nevertheless be made even when more time to obtain more facts would, in a perfect world, be preferable. Most important, never disregard or cover up a poor decision, but move forward based on the facts and circumstances to make the better decision.

The decision-making process can be analyzed, as follows:

- Suppress ego.

- Try, succeed.

- Try, fail, re-suppress ego, and try again.

- Take a few deep breaths, get some water, take a short walk, and clear the mind.

- Embrace the problem.

- Find a viable solution.

Ah, but we want and need those pesky little facts, some of which could have a course-altering impact. Yet, time sometimes just won't tolerate the luxury of obtaining more information.

Did you know that in every issue of *Investor's Business Daily*, the

Chapter 8 | THE NEGOTIATION OF MOTIVATION

newspaper prints its never-changing "IBD's 10 Secrets to Success?" The sixth secret is "Learn to analyze details; get all the facts, all the input. Learn from your mistakes." The tenth secret applies to the other nine, but is a corollary to the sixth. "Be honest and dependable; take responsibility."

We've discussed decision making and adjusting poor decisions. But how can we make the proper adjustment if we don't:

- Get all the facts, all the input,

- (so we can) learn from our mistakes.

Of course, to do so we must:

- Be honest about the poor decision.

- Work to show we are dependable, even in a difficult situation.

- Take responsibility (to improve the prior decision).

Surprisingly, it is often hard to take the time to get all the facts, even when they are presented to us. But why is this? It is because we hear them, but we are not listening, or because our emotions are embroiled by a prior problem, a future worry, or another currently pressing issue.

Let's see how we all suffer from these obstacles to getting all the facts in a scenario we've all encountered. Have you ever visited a strange city, in your country or elsewhere, and gotten lost? And did you ask a stranger for directions? Almost all of us have. How often did you hear and listen to each part of the direction? Did you ever write the directions on a piece of paper? Did you repeat the directions to be certain you heard them correctly? Did you? I doubt it. Why?

Let's replay this movie vignette of a moment in our lives. We probably were driving for some time before we allowed ourselves to not only think we might be lost but accept the fact that we needed help. Perhaps we were late for an important business appointment or for a surprise party. Hence, by the time we admitted to ourselves that we

65

needed help, we were under a certain degree of time-induced stress. The poor decision was already made. Actually, it was a series of poor decisions, each one ending in not seeking directions, thus delaying the inevitable decision. Hence, we now had to adjust these poor decisions with a good decision. Obtain directions. How simple!

Yet, the stress of the moment, exacerbated by the impending late arrival, caused us to dilute our good decision by failing to clarify the directions we just received and making sure we really got it. We were given all the facts and could ask questions to get all the input, but did we? When part of the direction was to make a right turn at the third light about seventeen miles away, did we ask for a guidepost so we would not miss it? Did we make sure it was a right and not a left turn? Did we ask for a sense of distances between directional changes?

Is it any different in a business context? Did we allow the stranger giving us directions to lull us into failing to get all the details when he started the directions with either, "It's easy" or "It's not far," or "You won't have any trouble finding the place?" Or perhaps it may have been in the business context, with your internal thoughts saying to you that "It's okay," "The client won't mind," "It was good enough."

This scenario, in which our emotions are slightly elevated due to the time pressure (think every workday), occurs all the time. We just don't realize it. Why? Because our mind is constantly bombarded by past trespasses and future concerns. Hence, we often skip the small stuff and fail to pay attention to the little details. We wallow in our self-pity which we sublimate to allow ourselves to justify the status quo. But it's often the little things that count. It's often the seemingly insignificant fact from our employee's perspective or a seemingly unimportant throw-away response from our customer which, when reflected upon, can provide critical clues and insights as to how to proceed. How easily we can fix things when we descend from our ego-filled perch and get back into the field to make the adjustments necessary by allowing ourselves to really see the facts as they exist at the moment.

We miss these little things, often the true tells of the situation, because we turned off. We turned off our ears because we think we've learned enough (that's our ego giving yet more bad advice). We've got the big picture; we now have a preconceived notion of how to proceed. So we skip the extra few minutes necessary to get all the details (there's that ego again). In the direction scenario, we then all too often end up asking yet another stranger for directions. Wandering forward, we learn from the second stranger that we must reverse ourselves, reverse course. We have not gone forward; we have not made progress. Not surprisingly, it's the lack of attention to details that causes wandering. And wandering is circular. It's the little facts and seemingly insignificant input that provide the directional markers, in all contexts, to reach our goal.

So remember what we all learned in grade school when we became old enough to leave the house on our own and cross the street. Stop, look, and listen. Stop thinking about distractions and focus on the matter at hand. Be in the present and take the few extra minutes to get all the facts. Hear not just with your ears, but also hear with your eyes. Best of all, hear with your entire being so you can really listen and get it. Most importantly, never let a mistake remain as is. Mistakes never die. They never completely go away. They may dissolve almost entirely with time, but they leave an imperceptible scar. They will fester. They will fester until fixed. Sometimes resolution requires a simple apology. Other times a restorative adjustment is required. Analyze your mistakes and fix them. Admit the error. Take responsibility for yourself and your team members. Make it a positive learning experience by making it right. In so doing, you let others know you are dependable and not afraid to take responsibility. When you fix your mistakes, the universe thanks you. While everyone in your universe may not thank you, your karma surely will!

PRACTICE POINTS

- Failure to make a decision is a decision. It's just a bad decision.

LAUNCHING!

- Decision making is hard. We fear mistakes.

- Decisions are generally part of a continuum. They are seldom static.

- Almost any decision can be adjusted.

- A decision to attend a school or take a job can be adjusted by transfer.

- Very few decisions are unchangeable.

- If we overcome our fear of fear and our fear of ridicule, we unleash our decision-making prowess.

Chapter 9
NEGOTIATION "WARM-UPS"

LAUNCHING!

A successful negotiator never loses sight of the goal—closing. Of course, not every deal should close, but successful negotiators close almost all their deals, and certainly more than expected. Moreover, they are able to close them on terms acceptable to them (or their boss or client) even though it might appear that the terms finally agreed upon are quite different than expected (with the skill of the negotiator playing a direct role in improving his principal's terms and/or finding acceptable compromises). How is it that a set of terms that would have been rejected at the outset of a deal become acceptable compromises? Have things changed that much between the initiation and resolution of a negotiation, or have we changed? Generally, it's the latter. What is it about us that's changed?

Usually, it's two-fold. First, the knowledge base of successful negotiators grows as the transaction progresses. Good negotiators become deal-smarter. Second, our preconceived notions of our "wants and needs" necessary for the deal to close often shift during the negotiations.

But is such a shift a good thing? Well, it depends. If we shift our positions based on new facts, better understanding, and less emotion, we will be making a more informed decision. If we can digest more information without emotionalizing, we can truly absorb the facts as they are, and really digest them. If we can neutralize our ego, we can see and hear the new information for what it really means. Remember, facts are like dry leaves. Emotion is the wind within us which will stir up, blow, and blur the dry, factual leaves. When we control our ego and our emotion, there is no wind. And, when the wind dies down, when

Chapter 9 | NEGOTIATION "WARM-UPS"

there is calm, we can really see the leafy facts. Controlled emotion, neutralized ego, is the predicate for a judicious reaction.

A good negotiator never loses sight of the goal. But exactly what is the goal? The goal is always to make the best attainable deal, given the facts, circumstances, and relative leverage of the parties, as you understand it. It's at that point that a good go–no go decision can be made on individual points of contention and the deal as a whole.

Yet such an apparently simple goal is elusive for many. Why? We allow our ego to confuse us, to cause us to see and hear facts not as they are, but as we perceive them. That is, if we are even listening at all. Our ego will cause us to personalize the issues—to even allow us to feel insulted—rather than work to understand the adversary's perceptions— his perceived needs and wants, and most important, his perception of what we are saying. What we think we are saying is almost irrelevant. What really counts is what our adversary thinks he heard. And, when our ego takes control, we stop working to understand the other side's concerns. We stop working to find solutions. We only see and hear our positions. At that point, the seeds of impasse grow.

Successful negotiators are fact finders. They know that deal intelligence is a function of intelligence gathering. The origin of the intelligence really doesn't matter. It can be gleaned from newspaper articles, Internet bloggers, or any other of the myriad sources of public information available from so many information outlets.

While successful negotiators will know that public information is the necessary predicate for a successful deal foundation, they also know that the real jewels of information are mined in listening to the adversary. It's usually the information developed from interpersonal communication that takes the negotiator to a higher level of understanding. The uplift that elevates our deal acumen, skill, and flexibility is usually a function of the information gleaned from the adversary, because it's the adversary's perception that counts. The adversary's perception of you, your leverage, his leverage, and the facts available are critical if you are to understand the other side so you can work to find compromise and

LAUNCHING!

solution. It's the adversary's perception regardless of the reality.

What kind of information is that? There are two types: objective and subjective. By asking questions, we obtain information, some of which is factual, some of which may be emotional and purely subjective. For example, during a rainstorm, a typical opening question to the other side when all first meet for the day's sit-down might be: "What do you think of the weather?" Let's examine two possible responses:

Response No. 1: It's awful ... I hated my commute.

Response No. 2: Pretty wet out there but I'm glad it's not snow—this amount of rain could have been over a six-inch snowstorm if it were a few degrees colder.

So what have we learned? Certainly nothing about the weather! We already knew the weather. So what information was the skillful negotiator seeking? What was learned?

First, we learned from Response No. 1:

- The respondent dislikes rain.

- Rain elongates his commute.

- He probably dislikes commuting.

- He may already be in a sour mood. Maybe the weather soured him, but maybe something else.

What can we deduce—what is our action plan?

- Regardless of the reason, his mood is not good.

- We can probe to see if it's the weather or his commute.

- If we are not sure it's the weather or his commute, we can try to uncover why he is in a sour mood—the real reason.

Second, we learned from Response No. 2:

- He may dislike snow, but he sees the bright side of a rainy day.

Chapter 9 | NEGOTIATION "WARM-UPS"

- Perhaps he has a better attitude for the day's negotiation and even life in general: a glass-half-full type of person.

Why? The snow part is easy. What's more interesting is the positive attitude about the weather. Or was it? Did you notice his tone, inflection, cadence, overall body movement, and usually most important, facial expression? Was it said in a gloomy, "it couldn't be worse tone" or a grateful, "it could have been worse" tone, or even a positive "thank goodness" tone? Did you notice what his tone, cadence, inflection, and body movements were telling you? Yes, they were all speaking to you. Did you get it? Were you paying attention? Were you diverted by your thoughts or because you were distracted by another person in the room?

You say, "Who cares?" You should care! But you think to yourself, "It's just filler with no importance," "It's just an amenity conversation to use as an icebreaker." Right, but wrong. You are right that the substance is relatively trivial (at least as long as the rainstorm doesn't intensify to the point of flooding), but you are wrong if you treat the conversation as a trivial warm-up. It's actually an important warm-up. It's the warm-up exercise of all of your senses. It's the warm-up of every part of your being to put yourself in the present moment, to focus so you can take in and absorb all that is occurring around you.

Focus requires the use of the "focus muscle." The one in your brain that blocks out distractions and allows you to be completely in the present, focusing on what you are seeing and hearing.

Focus requires a little calisthenics because it's so easy to be distracted. It's so easy to daydream. Perhaps it began while walking or driving to the meeting. Perhaps we arrived at the negotiation deep in thought or reflection. Maybe we are thinking about a forthcoming vacation or an upcoming dental visit necessitated by pain that is intermittent but just won't go away. Hence, good negotiators exercise their focus muscle as soon as they walk into the negotiating room. Even beforehand, they recognize the need to take the time to transition from their life's distractions—to temporarily divorce themselves from the distraction which is their life. They need to free themselves from other thoughts

LAUNCHING!

and focus on the matter at hand.

More important, they understand the little gems that can be gleaned while people are more at ease before the negotiation starts. They look for the tells that will create pressure points to be squeezed later during the negotiations. Perhaps the weather will cause the adversary to want to telescope the meeting, to get it done quickly. Knowing that creates an edge, a little advantage.

They recognize that to be flexible enough to make the deal will usually require much more information, much more input than is usually available at the outset. So good negotiators warm up their focus and attention muscles. It doesn't require jumping jacks or push-ups before the meeting, although a workout in the morning or a brisk walk to the meeting or taking the stairs rather than the elevator will all help. Rather, we warm up our focus and attention muscles by really listening to each and every word. We listen to the silence between words and listen for the silent period at the end of each sentence. The subject matter is irrelevant. The amenity conversation may be trivial, but you'll catch a nugget of information if it spills out, often an unintended disclosure by the speaker—a disclosure that the speaker hadn't even realized he made which you caught by focusing. Believe me, you've done it. We've all done it. Sometimes we just talk too much—and say too much. In fact, most of us say and reveal much more than we realize. Good negotiators always warm up so they can take advantage of those disclosures whenever they occur. The next chapter takes us from warm-ups to the final closing stretch.

PRACTICE POINTS

- Don't drag your personal problems into a negotiation. No one really cares (better to call your mom—she'll listen).

- Bring a positive attitude to all negotiations. It's infectious. It works.

- Be a listener.

- Knowledge is power and focus can reward you with additional valuable knowledge.

- Ask friendly questions and really listen to the response. Follow up with more friendly questions. It shows interest in and respect for the other person.

- Be a sponge. When others talk, help them to keep talking. Most of us often say and reveal too much. Why? Because we like to talk about ourselves. For most of us, it's our favorite subject.

- Perception is reality. Has the other person understood what you said as you intended? Have you understood what the other person said as they intended?

Chapter 10
THE CLOSING

LAUNCHING!

Few of us think of ourselves as closers. In fact, we all are—at least to a degree. We close transactions all the time. We just don't think of them as closings because they are usually small, sometimes insignificant, and of a fairly recurring nature.

Yet, with all that practice, why do we become flustered with the big ones? Simple—for the most part, we allow ourselves to become too emotionally invested. Of course, as humans, we cannot help that; it's natural. But becoming overly emotionally invested, while natural, is also harmful to our closing success, because when we become overly emotionally invested, we telegraph to the other side—the car dealer or the homeowner selling his home—that we'll pay more, because we emit the sense that we can't or don't want to live without it. Therefore, if we want to become better closers, more effective closers, we need to learn how to control our emotions.

You might say, "What can I do? I love the car. I love the house." Ah, the classic dilemma!

Now, in truth, it's really hard to control that emotion, especially when we fixate on what we have convinced ourselves is our dream car or our dream home. But, in fact, there is no such thing as only one dream car or only one dream home. Even if we are convinced that this is the one, why telegraph the emotion? The problem is often our emotional inability or unwillingness to look for another (car or house) within what are often artificial time constraints we have set for ourselves. Why do we allow time constraints, if artificial, to affect us so? Either because we didn't plan ahead and are now forced to act within a time frame that would have been longer had we begun our search earlier,

Chapter 10 | THE CLOSING

or because our emotions allow us to believe we can't wait any longer. Well, since there's no accounting for poor planning, we will leave true time constraints to the poor planners. Instead let's focus on those who convince themselves they are forced to act in a limited time frame but in fact would have more time had they not become emotionally over-invested and artificially reduced their time horizon.

How can those who find their dream car or dream home, but can't afford the terms, work to obtain closing terms they can afford? What are the techniques they must master to avoid the trap of "I can't live without it. I must have it today?" Let's see.

First, let's analyze the basis of the "can't live without it" syndrome. For the most part, it develops from falling in love with an inanimate object such as a car or a house, coupled with the ignorance that comes from the laziness of thinking there is no reason to spend any more time because there cannot be anything better in the relevant marketplace (*i.e.*, the predetermined areas in which you would like to live or to where you are willing to drive to visit a dealer).

But it's not just laziness. It's fear! It's the fear of finding something equal or better and having now created the dilemma of deciding between two choices, when no such decision was required before. In fact, the decision we make when electing to look no further is the decision not to work hard to expand our choices and the decision not to create the stress of having to make additional decisions.

Yet, our fear of having to make decisions, of complicating our life, is a negative on many levels. First, when we discontinue our search, we have accepted that we have found the best option. However, by definition, when we limit our options, we are inherently making a poor decision. Is it due to laziness, fear, or both?

Voluntary limiting of options is for the lazy and the insecure. Voluntary limitations bespeak an unwillingness to work harder, often a result of an insidious gut fear that the dream decision made on the facts at hand may in fact not be so. And, were we to find a better car or home, we would have to accept that our initial selection might be less than

LAUNCHING!

our best decision. Even more difficult, by creating a choice, we have to overcome our insecurity that we may not make the better selection between the two choices.

So how do we overcome these obstacles to obtain closing success? The first obstacle, laziness, is easy to overcome. Work a little bit harder, work a little bit smarter, work a little bit faster. Information wants to burst out of the Internet and stream into our consciousness. Our research effort is streamlined. The Internet has made it so easy.

On the other hand, the second is not easy. To avoid the "fear of choice" obstacle, we must first accept the notion that there are no "bests." None of us has the best doctor or the best lawyer or the best garage mechanic. We may think we do, to subliminally justify our use of the person, or because of our obvious ignorance. How can we possibly know if our doctor, lawyer, or mechanic is the best? The answer, of course, is not only that we can't, but also that, at best, he is only among the best. Why? The world is just that large—there are so many excellent professionals out there that no one in a population this large can be the best. If you don't believe me, think about this: did you ever wonder how it is that miraculous discoveries were often made by scientists in different parts of the world—on different continents—virtually simultaneously? Of course, the answer must be that there are many brilliant men and women working to solve the same or similar problems at the same time independent of each other. How many times have we heard about scientists around the world racing against each other to discover (and discovering at near or about the same time) a new particle in an atom, or a new element in the Periodic Table of the Elements, or not too long ago a new island or lake, even a new continent (remember Christopher Columbus)?

So how can it be that multiple dream cars and multiple dream houses do not exist for you? Of course they do!

Once we accept there is no best, no one dream car or dream house, and once we couple that acceptance with the constant search for other dream cars and other dream houses by overcoming any laziness and

Chapter 10 | THE CLOSING

neutralizing our fear of decision, we can be more successful closers.

Let's see how it might work. Assume after three months of looking, you find a house outside of your price range that you love. You'd like to stretch for it, but it's listed for sale too high. At this point, however, you are emotionally hooked. You and your spouse can surrender to your emotions and pay more than you can afford and perhaps buy more house than you need, or you can examine your emotionalism and, therefore, see the situation differently.

What can you do? You need to think differently. You need to re-set your thought process so you can re-set your approach and execute a plan to help bring the house into your price range.

Start by saying to each other there is no one best house. There are many best houses, you simply need to find them or act as if you have found at least one more. How?

You must work harder and, if you are using a real estate agent, have him work harder. You must believe there are other houses that are just as good, or even better. Even if your dream house is within your price range, you will still obtain a better price if you allow yourself to believe there are other dream houses available. In fact, there almost always are.

Now, you say your spouse told you that if you procrastinate and lose the purchase, he or she will "kill" you. That's a tough one, and it's hard to overcome in a seller's market. But, while price-exploding bubbles will always recur—it's built into the fabric of our human nature (remember the tulip bulb market bubble, which reached its height in the winter of 1637 in Holland?)—they don't occur that often. In fact, good common sense, rational analysis, and a supportive spouse, except during those infrequent irrational bubble periods, will win the day.

The next step is execution. Do you just ask your agent to help you keep looking? If your agent is an expert in all of the areas that appeal to you, one agent will suffice. But, that's unlikely. Why not, in all events, tell your agent to review with you all the listings of the listing agent who represents the seller of the house you love? Are you uncomfortable asking your agent to do the extra work? Will you allow the agent to

LAUNCHING!

dissuade you from the additional investigation? Why? It's business. You don't need to have your agent fall in love with you and your spouse. You need your agent to earn the commission. Since the listing agent had one dream house in his inventory that you loved, maybe there are others. There may not be a more effective way to nudge a seller than to view other homes listed by the seller's agent. Maybe even act as if you like them. In fact, allow yourself to like them and you may surprise yourself. That's right! Allow yourself to even feign liking another house. It's not illegal, immoral, or fattening. Perhaps you will recognize another house as better—and even if it's not, it's a great negotiating tactic. Why? Because it works. By convincing yourself other homes are as good or even better, you will emit that sense of assuredness and security that the first home you like is just one of many. Believe me, it works. I've used the technique more than once.

So you say it's too much work and too much stress and tension for you and your spouse. It's surely extra work and it's surely an added degree of stress and tension, but allowing yourself to believe it's too much work or too much stress and tension is an emotional failure. There is no such thing as too much stress or too much tension. There is only too much if we allow ourselves to believe it's too much. Secretaries get just as stressed as their executive-suite bosses. Stress is a function of our lack of belief in ourselves, and our inability to believe that we can perform, that we can prevail, and that we can be successful; most importantly, it is a failure of belief in the fact that we can "just do it," to borrow a successful marketing phrase from Nike.

In fact, we can all perform and we can all prevail. The human condition allows for stresses of all types and kinds, even incredible pain. When we think about children fighting to survive in Africa or combat veterans returning with missing limbs, handling stress in easier circumstances is just a walk in the park. Treat it as such and succeed.

PRACTICE POINTS

- Successful closers are fact seekers.

- More information points make for greater options and more informed choices.

- Never let fear rob you of creating more options. Life will foreclose options without your help.

- Never foreclose your options voluntarily.

- Force yourself to create a decision tree. You can always revert to your first choice, particularly if additional information supports your first choice as the best choice.

- Speak less and listen more.

Chapter 11

NEGOTIATING TECHNIQUES

FOR LEADERS AND THEIR LAWYERS – ATTITUDE AND FOCUS

LAUNCHING!

Effective negotiators understand that a negotiation provides the opportunity for building a relationship, a relationship which may last for one short meeting, or perhaps several meetings over several days, weeks, or months. The relationship may be short-lived, long-term, or may even blossom into a lifelong friendship. By recognizing that negotiating, in essence, is the formation and development of relationships, the most effective negotiators are able to obtain what they need, and much—or most—of what they want, while nevertheless ceding to the adversary the "gives" necessary to reach the compromises for successful resolution. Effective negotiators are deal makers. They are neither deal breakers nor, worse, litigation makers.

Negotiation may be a relationship with an adversary for whom you dislike or distrust. Nevertheless, at least until the negotiation is concluded, a relationship will exist by virtue of participating with each other in negotiations which will result in either successful conclusion or unsuccessful termination. Why not seek to enhance it? Why not try to understand the adversary's perspective? Why not try to gain the adversary's trust?

Of course, the direction from the beginning of negotiations to the end may not be a straight line—negotiations may be interrupted or simply stall because of an exogenous event, yet eventually revitalize. Some have said that almost no deals are forever dead. Regardless of their unlikelihood, some set of facts might, were they to occur with the necessary sequencing and timing, revive the negotiations and lead to a successful conclusion.

The point is as simple in its validity as it is clear in its benefits.

Chapter 11 | NEGOTIATING TECHNIQUES – FOR LEADERS AND THEIR LAWYERS – ATTITUDE AND FOCUS

Negotiations are, in fact, relationships. It may not be necessary to conduct them over a campfire with s'mores; on the other hand, they need not be bare-knuckle events with gamesmanship and gotchas. Such tactics bespeak an out-of-control ego on one or both sides which will only hinder the goals of both clients—resolution of the open issues without killing the deal or, worse, resorting to litigation. Negotiating strength usually manifests itself best through the use of grace and kindness. Table-pounding seldom works even if you use your shoe. Just ask Nikita Khrushchev, former leader of the former Soviet Union.

Before proceeding further, let's consider negotiation with an adversary we already dislike or distrust. Are we really upset with the adversary? Or does our negative attitude emanate from elsewhere? Why do we have a case of pre-meeting negative attitude? Perhaps a problem at home or the inconvenience of the time or day of the meeting, or our sense of frustration because we believe the other side is inexperienced or lacks authority to make decisions. Regardless of the source of irritation or frustration, neutralize it! It's a negative attitude. Change it! Put on your deal-maker attitude. Just change your "attitude clothes." To paraphrase Thoreau, we are what we think.

On the other hand, let's assume you arrive at the meeting with a positive deal-maker's attitude, but upon arrival, you are bombarded by the other side with a demeaning and cavalier attitude. What should you do? You can allow the barbs to pierce your ego and react in kind, or you can elect not to react. Which do you think will be more effective? Which option will likely produce the better atmosphere for a successful negotiation? And which response will provide the better platform for you if and when you need to momentarily take the gloves off to win a key point?

The negotiation of any matter offers many opportunities to meld legal knowledge and skills with business acumen, all overlaid with creativity. Some negotiators simply run through all or some of the issues, basically accepting that which the other side is willing to offer with respect to

LAUNCHING!

each and every issue. Such an approach is not negotiation at all. It is capitulation. On the other hand, the good negotiator recognizes that a negotiation usually has many stages with pressures and pressure points appearing, vanishing, and reappearing in various intensities during each stage. The skilled negotiator attempts, at all times, to direct which issues and pressure points will be focused upon and whether they will be individualized, linked to another issue, or aggregated. Each aspect of the negotiation provides opportunities to exercise skill, knowledge, and creativity.

Listening

Before discussing the techniques and devices that follow, a few words about the seminal skill of negotiating—listening. Mastering the skill of listening is fundamental to becoming a skillful negotiator. Listening can be defined as using all of our senses to understand what the other person, your adversary, is saying. Listening is hard to do well (in fact, so hard that I wrote a book about it).

In short, if the adversary does not perceive we are listening to him, trying to understand not just what he is saying, but what he means, how can we expect to gain his trust? How can we expect him, in turn, to listen to us when we speak? We can't. Why should he? Would you? How do you feel when you sense someone is not listening to you? Probably somewhat slighted. But when you are speaking, how can you tell that you don't have another's focus and attention? We all can tell. It's easy. Let's list some of the telltale signs—the "tells"—that signal another person is not really listening. They are so obvious. All we need to do is observe as we speak. For example:

1. Is there eye contact from the listeners?

2. Does their posture indicate that they are really focusing?

3. Are there fidgets or similar seemingly small and minor body movements indicating an unease, disapproval, or lack of

Chapter 11 | NEGOTIATING TECHNIQUES – FOR LEADERS AND THEIR LAWYERS – ATTITUDE AND FOCUS

interest in what we are saying?

4. Do they interrupt before we finish our sentence or thought?

5. Do they respond simultaneously with the drop in our voice just as we are concluding a sentence?

The list can be continued, but let's take a closer look at the fifth point: jumping in within a nanosecond of the end of the speaker's comment. That's not rude - the fourth point is rude, an obvious interruption, a cut off. The fifth point is not as obvious as the fourth, but it's just as much a tell that the other side isn't listening, or stopped listening, or doesn't want to listen to you. How do I know? I know because we think at a speed far in excess of the speed at which we speak. An interruption in mid-sentence or a jump-in at the end of a sentence indicates that the listener was forming a response while we were still speaking, rejecting, in whole or in part, what we were saying. If he was thinking about his position and wanting to present it as soon as possible, how could he have been listening to us, really understanding what we were saying, really trying to get it? We know he couldn't be, because we know that we are not listening, or have stopped listening, when we are preparing to interrupt the speaker or be the first to jump in and speak at the slightest pause.

You may say you can multitask. You can listen to someone speak and formulate your response at the same time. Maybe, just maybe, you can. However, I assure you that, even if you can, your adversary will not think so. And his perception of your interest in what he has to say is what counts. Your perception of you is irrelevant. Go tell it to your ego (but more about ego later).

So what can you do, or what should you do, to become a better negotiator? It's simple. Listen. Really listen. Listen for the silence at the end of another's comments. Then, let silence reign for two or three seconds, and only then respond. What have you just accomplished?

LAUNCHING!

Let's see. You showered your adversary's comments with respect. You said, through your patience and silence, that what the other person had to say was important enough for you to really listen to, and even reflect upon, before you responded. Isn't that the way to develop a relationship and begin to create a sense of trust?

But wait. There's more. There can be incredible benefits to being polite, gracious, and a gifted listener. Why? Because many of us throw in end-of-sentence nuggets of information which often provide the true meaning of what the speaker is saying and/or feeling. These types of comments are often accompanied by a laugh or a nervous gesture. Psychologists might tell us the gesture is a screen to hide the speaker's discomfort in disclosing his true feeling or position. Of course, you will never hear those seemingly innocuous little end-of-sentence chuckles, comments, or asides if you jump in on a split-second basis, or worse, interrupt.

But wait! There's still more. By waiting a few moments before responding to another's comments, you allow silence to fill the room. In a sense, you are creating a vacuum. And, just as nature abhors a vacuum and seeks to fill it, so, too, most of us are uncomfortable with silence and tend to fill it. We tend to fill it with words. And, as often as not, the words spoken during the awkward moments of silence are tells into the true meaning and intent of the speaker.

So take the high road of great listeners. Learn to truly focus on the speaker. Focus on the words, inflection, intonation, cadence, and body movement. Why? Because we all say more than we think. Very few of us can hide all of our emotions and all of our feelings all of the time during a negotiation.

Interestingly, most of us tend to say too much and disclose more than we think. If we accept that premise, we should develop techniques to keep them talking. But how? That's easy. Just ask questions. Do your homework. Pose thoughtful questions. Then follow up with clarifying questions. If you ask the questions without injecting your ego, and without condescension or disdain, your adversary will perceive you are

Chapter 11 | NEGOTIATING TECHNIQUES – FOR LEADERS AND THEIR LAWYERS – ATTITUDE AND FOCUS

really working hard to understand his position.

Questions are like drills. The deeper you drill, the more likely you'll hit pay dirt, and the more likely you'll hear that new fact or true intent or find that other vein of gold that has yet to be discovered. Asking questions is an art and a science. It's a science because good questions develop from a thorough understanding of the topic or subject matter. It's an art because any given answer may create a dead end. The skilled negotiator knows how to avoid dead-ends and look for a different route. It requires a good understanding of the topic and the ability to be quick on one's feet. For example, a "no" might seem like a dead end, and further questions after hearing a no may seem rude to some. But, in fact, no is only the first part of a sentence. The second part of the sentence starts with the word "because." Skilled negotiators know how to tease out the rest of that sentence. Sometimes, it's as simple as saying, "Can you give me a reason?" Other times, the skilled negotiator may humanize the interchange, a concept discussed later, by saying, "Please don't ask me to go back with a flat-out no—give me some basis, share your thinking with me, so I don't appear foolish to my client (boss, spouse, fill in the blank)."

PRACTICE POINTS

- Every negotiation is the formation of a relationship, regardless of duration.

- Effective negotiators are good listeners.

- Never interrupt.

- Listen for the silent period at the end of a speaker's sentence.

- Use silence to learn more—to allow for the unintended disclosure.

LAUNCHING!

- Never allow the bad mood of your adversary to affect you—maintain a positive attitude.

Chapter 12

NEGOTIATING TECHNIQUES

FOR LEADERS AND THEIR LAWYERS – PREPARATION

LAUNCHING!

Preparation is the springboard for negotiating success.

For illustrative purposes, for the balance of this and the following two chapters, we will assume an attorney-client negotiating team. Oftentimes, attorneys assume they are prepared simply by having a thorough grounding in the various areas of the law that will be touched upon during the negotiation. However, that attitude can be both naïve and foolish. For a successful negotiation, equally critical as knowledge of the law is knowledge of the client's needs and concerns and those of the adversary. Accordingly, once armed with a thorough understanding of the substantive areas of the relevant law, a good attorney-negotiator thinks through the various positions that might be taken with respect to whatever issues are expected to be deal points.

But how does a good attorney-negotiator learn, or better understand, the business issues of his client and the adversary? It requires homework. It requires studying the business of one's client and of one's adversary. It may require reading trade journals and relevant newspaper articles. It absolutely requires reading the material available about each party's business. If either or both companies are publicly traded, the amount of publicly accessible material is, at first blush, voluminous. But at least, each company's annual report should be studied, as well as recent quarterly reports and material event reports. All of the information is readily available on Securities and Exchange Commission Forms 10-K, 10-Q, and 8-K. But, what if neither company is publicly traded? We can read through each company's website, but is that really enough?

Chapter 12 | NEGOTIATING TECHNIQUES – FOR LEADERS AND THEIR LAWYERS – PREPARATION

Probably not. So, let's go the extra mile. Determine the industry segment of each company, and select a leading, publicly traded company in each segment. Then, simply obtain the SEC documents for those companies. You'll be surprised how quickly you will become well grounded in the issues affecting your client and the adversary. Armed with this information, not only may you discover pressure points, but your ability to talk shop will be enhanced. In so doing, you might be pleasantly surprised in the tidbits you may learn from a discussion of general business conditions affecting each party's business, especially the adversary's. Remember, most people's favorite topic is themselves, followed closely by their business. Get the adversary talking. Most of us, even the best of us, once talking about ourselves or our business, usually say too much. The irony is we seldom realize it. If you don't believe me, think back to the last time someone asked you, "How did you know that about me?" and your answer or thought was, "You told me!"

Once grounded in the relevant business, good attorney-negotiators mentally playact the various strategies and positions that might be employed with respect to any issue or term considered a negotiation point. By preparing in this manner, the attorney is not preconditioned to the client's needs, wants, and desires. By free-thinking each issue, the effective attorney-negotiator can often create additional approaches to an issue, additional satisfactory resolutions for the client, and ultimately, more effective compromise positions so that both parties can reach consensus and move to the next point. Failing to analyze and internalize each point prior to meeting with the client may cause the attorney to be over-influenced by the client and to be hampered by the same blinders the client is wearing. Therefore, diligent attorneys perform this free-think analysis prior to and after the initial discussion of the issues with the client.

Team negotiations, without having first met in person, should be avoided whenever possible. Even if the negotiators have discussed the

LAUNCHING!

issues on the phone, it is still advantageous to meet in person, even for a few minutes—in the waiting room of the adversary's office before the meeting, or over a cup of coffee prior to the meeting—to obtain a feel for the other's in-person demeanor. Since negotiation involves a certain degree of playacting, it is worthwhile for the attorney and the client to get an understanding of each other's body language and face-to-face personality.

By meeting either in person or on the phone—preferably multiple times—the attorney improves his ability to understand the real needs and concerns of the client and can thereby help the client develop or adjust the final position on many of the issues. Free-thinking creates an open mind. Ironically, an objective perspective is often one of the key reasons attorneys are retained, *i.e.*, to offer intelligent and creative objectivity to a particular situation and to aid the client's rethinking of positions and reevaluation of potential trade-offs. Clients are more effective when they better understand the relative value of different issues, and, equally important, which issues may be more valuable to the adversary. By better understanding the relative values of deal points to each side, the client can employ his arsenal of giveaways more effectively. Effective clients expect and demand this dynamic; the ineffective ones prefer yes-men.

An open mind flexes the negotiation muscles and keeps them limber. Flexibility is often critical to a successful negotiation. Flexibility is often the ingredient necessary to allow a successful compromise—a compromise where the point the client has ceded is less valuable than the point won—which is still a win for both sides. Analyzing the needs and concerns of the opposition is so important. It's a difficult analysis on many levels since we can never know what the other side is truly thinking, but it is shortsighted to neglect the other side's needs and concerns. By understanding the relative value of deal points to both sides, the effective negotiator creates trade-offs of greater value.

Skilled negotiators play out and internalize various aspects of the negotiation for another reason, also. While mental playacting allows

Chapter 12 | NEGOTIATING TECHNIQUES – FOR LEADERS AND THEIR LAWYERS – PREPARATION

the negotiator to think through the issues, it also enables the negotiator to internalize responses. By so doing, statements can be comfortably made, and positions comfortably taken, with a tone of sincerity, legitimacy, and resolve in the ensuing dynamic, even though the other side may consider them outlandish or overreaching. Even if they are outlandish or overreaching, effective presentation hinders the adversary's ability to disregard them. It is virtually impossible to over-prepare for a negotiation.

Venue Strategy

While the concept of "home territory" can be overplayed (who must travel farthest), in certain circumstances it is important. In general, most of us believe it to be a sign of strength to insist that the opposition meet at our office or the office of our client. However, before discussing meeting location with respect to control and other dynamics, let's consider meeting location from a tonal perspective. Clearly, a meeting at a lawyer's office around a large, heavy wooden table with pictures of dead presidents on the wall is more formal than a meeting in a lunchroom, or a diner or restaurant. Whether or not the meeting room has windows can also affect the tone. In other words, the setting of the meeting can set the tone of the meeting. There are many reasons to have a formal setting as opposed to an informal setting, and it should be considered carefully. Whenever possible, match the setting of the meeting with the intended tone. Of course, this may not be practical.

Having discussed the setting, let's consider meeting venue strategy. Most of us do not consider it necessary to stand on formality and demand the meeting take place at our office. On the other hand, this can sometimes be an easy victory. While perhaps unimportant to all initially, it can nevertheless furnish value. A meeting in your home office is convenient. But more important, a meeting at the negotiator's office is that much easier for the negotiator to control. While control generally falls in the hands of the stronger and more skilled negotiator

LAUNCHING!

regardless of venue, a negotiator can enhance the ability to obtain or regain control by simply sitting at the head of the table, or by sitting next to the only conference phone in the meeting room, or by sitting nearest to the door. Control is often obtained initially by simply commencing the actual negotiation, *i.e.*, commencing the business parts of the meeting as differentiated from the pre-negotiation social pleasantries.

But remember, control is not a baton with which the next runner speeds off. Rather, it is a bouncing ball and can be retained or relinquished and regained at various times in a negotiation. Counterintuitively, it is not necessary to maintain control at all times or at any time during the negotiation so long as one understands why one has or does not have control. Sometimes, passing the control ball is a strength move. Learning how and when to pass control is incredibly valuable.

Therefore, let's spend a few minutes discussing passing techniques. Not to worry, no further sports analogy is coming. This is not basketball. It's negotiating psychology. So let's analyze a circumstance for a passing of control. Let's assume the parties have met before and are now meeting again to resolve an important issue which left the parties at an impasse. Let's further assume that you and your client cannot make any further concessions but the adversary remains unsatisfied and unwilling to accept your last offer. Nevertheless, since both clients want the issue resolved and the deal completed, you are meeting again. Once the pleasantries, or perhaps lack thereof in this case, are concluded, what are your options? What should you do?

You can:

- Offer up an apparent solution from your side and explain why your client cannot agree to it in clear, cogent terms (a "negative" pass of control).

- Suggest a solution from the other side and explain (rationalize) why they should agree to it (a "positive" pass of control).

Chapter 12 | NEGOTIATING TECHNIQUES – FOR LEADERS AND THEIR LAWYERS – PREPARATION

- Simply verbalize the stalemate and seek a solution from the other side (a "negative" pass of control).

- Verbalize the stalemate and demand a particular solution from the other side (a "positive" pass of control).

- Remain stone-faced (a "negative" pass of control).

- Explain how much progress both sides have made, how close the parties are to consummating a deal, and how both sides seek the same result—a successful conclusion.

Then, turn to the other side and prod them for a solution since, you argue:

- They are better positioned and have more insight.

- They are more experienced.

- They have more maneuvering room.

- Or whatever other compliment your creativity can conjure (all "positive" passes of control).

Passes of control are strength moves, perhaps positive passes of control more so than negative passes. But does it really matter? Perhaps to your ego, but we know that our ego, unchecked, is not our friend; rather, our nemesis.

Preopening pleasantries are seen as gracious behavior. But they can be much more. They can be piercing icebreakers used by the skilled negotiator to carefully observe and listen in order to ferret out a fact or emotion not intended to be disclosed. In addition, they can be used to "humanize" the meeting. However, the negotiator with greater leverage may seek to minimize the humanization factor and maintain a strong sense of formality. In fact, some negotiators intentionally skip the pleasantries in order to increase the tension and reduce the opposition's

LAUNCHING!

comfort level. Why?

Because, as people become transactionally friendly, the weaker side may feel it can take liberties (make "asks") greater than its leverage would warrant. Accordingly, expanding the preopening pleasantry aspect of a transaction may be an effective tool for the side who has little or no bargaining strength, or the lesser leverage. However, regardless of leverage, the skilled negotiator uses this period as a potential learning opportunity because most tend to speak more freely in the pleasantry period before the actual negotiations begin. As a result, the keen observer and focused listener often obtains valuable information and insights, whether by sight or sound, that the other side does not even realize it is disclosing. SUCCESSFUL NEGOTIATORS ARE EXCELLENT LISTENERS AND CAREFUL OBSERVERS. Disclosures by the adversary need not be momentous. In fact, it's often the little things that make the difference. Sometimes, just a seemingly inconsequential fact such as a time constraint or other pressure on the other side can be artfully used by the negotiator. Beyond picking up unintended disclosures by the adversary, the preopening pleasantries have a tactical use as well. A skilled negotiator may use this time to say informally that which might be offensive or virtually impossible to say during the more formal actual negotiations part of the meeting.

For example, a negotiator with leverage desiring to exhibit even greater strength might indicate, in casual conversation, that his client would like to make the deal but is prepared to pass; he might follow that comment with a rationale. Perhaps he could say the deal is only one of several of a similar nature, any of which would make sense and be sufficient for his client. Then to assuage the adversary's pique, he might indicate that the adversary's deal is slightly more appealing so he'd prefer it in lieu of the others. In a similar vein, the negotiator might say that his client privately indicated that he can make no further concessions and is meeting solely as a courtesy. Of course, the tactics available to the negotiator are only limited by the existing facts and the negotiator's creativity. Naturally, if the negotiator makes a statement,

Chapter 12 | NEGOTIATING TECHNIQUES – FOR LEADERS AND THEIR LAWYERS – PREPARATION

formally or informally, intended to "freeze" a position, it will be much more effective if supported by logical reasoning and underlying facts.

Returning to the concept of control, initial control is taken by the individual who terminates the preopening pleasantries. The pleasantries are concluded by simply commencing the meeting, moving from the pleasantry stage to the initial discussion stage, or the initial deal point. Any party may do so. Doing so puts initial control into the hands of the person making the statement. Why? Because, unless challenged, that person is selecting the starting point (the initial deal discussion point). Starting points can be critical. Even if not agreed to, the proactive negotiator at least has selected the initial skirmish line. Perhaps this line is an issue he knows will early test the other side's strength, cohesion, and resolve. On the other hand, he may select an initial issue readily susceptible to resolution because he wants to immediately inject "deal glue" into the negotiation. Obviously, tactics will vary based on the actual and perceived leverage of each side with respect to any deal point and with respect to the overall deal.

Once negotiations start, they may tend to lurch in various directions depending on the nature, complexity, and criticality of the issues discussed. It is generally in the beginning that strength is exercised and weakness exposed. It is in the beginning that the agenda is usually set, the parties agreeing upon the manner in which they are going to work through the deal points. Oftentimes, a discussion ensues regarding the sequence and placement of the big issues. When will they be addressed? Sometimes they are reserved until the end; other times, they are addressed first. Good negotiators usually play to their deal strengths early on by asserting, presenting, and continuously underscoring themes and concepts they wish to have permeate the entire negotiation.

PRACTICE POINTS

- Good negotiators prepare—they don't "wing it."

LAUNCHING!

- Good negotiators always engage in free-think analysis to help them better understand all the deal points from the perspective of both sides.

- Good negotiators are excellent listeners and careful observers.

- Good negotiators start focusing before they enter the negotiating room, and never allow themselves to lose focus.

Chapter 13

NEGOTIATING TECHNIQUES

FOR LEADERS AND THEIR LAWYERS – TACTICS

LAUNCHING!

Opening tactics are only limited by a negotiator's skill and creativity. One tactic is the start-real-hard-no-matter-what approach. This tactic uses initial aggression and purposefully puts the negotiation near or at the brink of falling apart by taking intractable stances on every issue raised. The strategy seeks to expose the adversary's concern with getting the deal done as well as the adversary's weaknesses. At a later point (minutes or hours or days), this tactic is softened by use of a more conciliatory attitude coupled with concessions which may then be accepted with greater appreciation than would otherwise be accorded.

Another tactic is the casual good-guy approach used to camouflage extremely hard-nosed positions on the issues. This tactic permits the negotiator to be a super-tough advocate on the issues, while nevertheless being an otherwise good guy who is only "forced" to take hard positions because the client so demands.

Many other early-stage tactics are available, including artificial contraction and artificial expansion of the negotiations. Sometimes, it may be in the best interest of the negotiator to make certain that all deal points are not resolved in one meeting. On the other hand, it may be in the best interest of the negotiator to force discussion and resolution of all the deal points in a single meeting. Similarly, it may be effective to appear to want to resolve all the deal points in one meeting, while nevertheless always intending to leave key selected points unresolved. This technique might be used when the negotiator believes that his leverage with respect to some points will increase after resolving certain other points. Techniques regarding speed and emphasis are, of course,

Chapter 13 | NEGOTIATING TECHNIQUES – FOR LEADERS AND THEIR LAWYERS – TACTICS

subject to the variables of each situation.

Another opening technique is to create confrontation on every issue (as opposed to providing varying degrees of opposition, or none at all); yet, unlike the earlier example, this technique presents no feigned or actual willingness to kill the deal. There may be reasons to do so. For example, this will telegraph a long and arduous negotiation. On the other hand, there are reasons to create the opposite impression and perhaps lull the other side into what they believe will be an easy negotiation, only later reversing tactics in order to create frustration by applying more pressure in subsequent calls and meetings. Much can be accomplished by picking and choosing the order in which issues are discussed. Initial control can be critical, even though any agenda can be reset or adjusted.

As is the case with the entire negotiating process, the initial aspect of negotiation is an orchestration, oftentimes filled with playacting and creation of impressions. It is at this point that the bromide, "There is only one chance to make a first impression," applies. A skillful negotiator may create impressions that may not appear to be in the client's best interest of closing the deal—hence, the importance of one or more meetings between the negotiator and client, either on the phone or, preferably, in person. The client needs to understand when the tactics and strategy are real or just bluffs. It is very difficult and often impossible to create impasse, or even slow down, without first obtaining the client's approval. Very few clients are willing to risk a deal and most clients dislike delay. It is important, therefore, for the negotiator to explain to the client that he has no intention of killing or stalling a deal. Rather, the negotiator is using these obstructionist tactics to obtain better resolution of issues than might otherwise be obtained. Of course, the client may indicate that if certain minimums cannot be obtained on key deal points, the client is prepared to kill, or at least postpone, the deal. In a sense, these situations are the easiest because the negotiator has a clear position, a so-called minimum get, to keep the deal from aborting.

But is such a circumstance really that easy for the negotiator? Only if the negotiator obtains the client's minimums. On the other hand, however, when the opposition's offer is below the client's minimum, the skilled negotiator must really get to work. Why? Because clients can change their mind; they may not mean what they say, and they may not say what they really mean. It's allowed. Why? Because they are the client. Therefore, a skilled negotiator understands that the client's minimum is not just a deal killer (if the adversary's offer falls short), but also a hurdle he must get the adversary to overcome. Why? Because skilled negotiators are not deal breakers, skilled negotiators are deal makers. Skilled negotiators deliver the best deal they can and offer the client the option of acceptance or rejection.

Just as the negotiator's mettle is put to the test when the adversary refuses to meet the deal-breaker minimum, it is also put to the test on the many less critical issues that permeate a negotiation. With those issues, which are not deal killers, the skillful negotiator shines by obtaining better terms than his actual leverage might suggest, simply by using the variety of tools and techniques available.

More Tactics and Techniques

While the opposition should never be underestimated, most of us are generally unwilling to spend the time—or endure the continuous confrontation—that long and difficult transactions require. It is in the nature of most of us to seek compromise and non-confrontational approaches. It is this element of human nature that the skilled negotiator may exploit by creating confrontation and prolonging negotiations. Then, the negotiator's subsequent gestures of conciliation are better received and perceived. Oftentimes, the combination of confrontation and conciliation enables the skilled negotiator to improve his client's position. Another technique is to postpone issues where the negotiator has the least leverage, only raising them when all of

Chapter 13 | NEGOTIATING TECHNIQUES – FOR LEADERS AND THEIR LAWYERS – TACTICS

the participants seek compromise and acceleration. This approach may permit the negotiator to aggregate or "bucket" issues where he or she is weakest to obtain better terms on some of the weaker positions. Sometimes this can be accomplished simply by employing Solomon's approach of suggesting to split the baby down the middle, awarding half of the issues to one side and the other half to the other side. Individualizing, versus linking, versus aggregating issues should be carefully analyzed at each stage of the negotiation as the dynamic of the negotiation and leverage of the parties' shifts.

As the negotiation progresses and positions are further developed, personalities better understood, and hot buttons more clearly discerned, additional tactics become available. An effective technique is the use of a theme. This technique can be employed in many ways. For example, pick a theme that is particularly important to the client and negotiate hard on every issue that touches upon the theme. Simply by declaring a particular theme as being of primary importance to the client, the negotiator is able to fare better on every issue touching the theme. A thematic position is strengthened to the degree that it is valid, and a valid theme enhances the negotiator's leverage on every issue involving the theme.

One overarching theme, for example, is the speed with which the deal must be completed. The negotiator may declare, as early as the telephone or e-mail exchanges setting up the initial meeting, that time is critical and the deal must be completed as quickly as possible. This conveys a sense that delay will kill the client's appetite to complete the deal, or that delay may allow competing deals to monopolize the client's attention. This device is best employed by the party with greater leverage. However, it is also effectively used by a negotiator who knows or believes his client's leverage will erode with the passage of time.

Another overarching theme, usable in virtually any down-payment, purchase-sale context, is collateral security. If a portion of the purchase

LAUNCHING!

price is being deferred, the skilled negotiator can often manufacture issues dealing with collateral security. Clearly, collateral security is a legitimate issue whenever a purchase price is not paid fully at closing. How can the opposition effectively argue the seller is not entitled to collateral security if a portion of the purchase price is deferred? The only issues about which the opposition can argue are the type and amount of the collateral, not if any collateral is appropriate.

"Theme-atics" (or "theme-antics") provides the negotiator with a leg up on all issues embraced by the theme. The theme becomes the gift that keeps on giving for the creative negotiator. Why? Because use of a theme not only adds legitimacy to issues surrounding the theme, it also allows the skilled negotiator to create additional deal points. Let's see.

For example, assume Mr. Buyer is purchasing the retail pizza business of your client, Mr. Seller, for $10 million. Mr. Seller must make a lot of pizzas. He does! He owns a chain of 500 pizza stores throughout the East Coast. Let's also assume that Mr. Buyer is paying $5 million at the closing, and paying the $5 million balance in five equal annual installments of $1 million. Let's further assume that the letter of intent that both men signed allows Mr. Seller to recover his business if Mr. Buyer defaults on the deferred payments. With this information, the attorney for the seller will focus intensely on getting Mr. Seller even more protection than just recovering the business for Mr. Seller if Mr. Buyer defaults. Why? Because Mr. Seller's attorney did his homework. He learned that used pizza equipment has little value. He also knows that Mr. Seller will use the sale proceeds to start an unrelated business. Hence, Mr. Seller's attorney will focus on assuring that his client is paid. But, Mr. Buyer already agreed to return the business if he defaulted. So what else can the seller's attorney ask for? Under the theme of collateral security, he can ask for anything he can think of to ensure Mr. Seller is paid. How can Mr. Buyer's attorney question his client's agreement to pay the entire purchase price? He can't. Nor can he question Mr. Seller's right to be paid in full.

But let's assume Mr. Seller tells his attorney he trusts Mr. Buyer and

Chapter 13 | NEGOTIATING TECHNIQUES – FOR LEADERS AND THEIR LAWYERS – TACTICS

is comfortable with a promissory note for the balance of the purchase price, together with a so-called security agreement (and filed UCC-1). Nevertheless, Mr. Seller's attorney can ask for:

- A co-maker(s) of the note

- Joint and several liability

- One or more guarantors

- Joint and several and co-primary liability for the guarantors

- A bank-issued letter of credit

- Maybe even Mr. Buyer's firstborn (of course, a bad idea if college, and the attendant tuition, is in the child's future)

The elegance of these asks is their inherent legitimacy (maybe not the last one). It really doesn't matter if Mr. Seller wants any or all of them. It's even better if he doesn't (that will facilitate trade-offs). Regardless, Mr. Seller's attorney can employ the complementary devices of creative issue-establishment and issue giveaway. In this scenario, the knowledgeable and creative negotiator has developed trade-away deal points. In so doing, the negotiator can trade away a lesser deal point (perhaps one he never thought he would win) created by his knowledge and ingenuity. Perhaps, in the trade, he wins an entirely different but important point. The elegance of the tactic applies even if the point traded for is not significant. Why? Because the point ceded was never a real deal issue. It only became real by virtue of being a tag-along to the quite credible and legitimate theme of ensuring payment by use of collateral security. This technique is extremely useful. It allows the skilled negotiator to raise the level of lesser deal points because of the inherent validity of the concept to which they are attached. In so doing, the value of the trade-off may increase. It is a win-win dynamic for the negotiator.

LAUNCHING!

But remember, it's all about the homework. In order to derive the full benefit of this tactic, the negotiator must thoroughly understand the business as well as the legal aspects of his client's endeavors. Then he can understand the relative importance of all of the deal points, be able to enhance lesser points, and trade some or all for more important or valuable other points.

PRACTICE POINTS

- Good negotiators always do their homework.

- Good negotiators free-think the transaction in order to create additional deal points to increase their client's leverage and flexibility.

- Good negotiators focus on all the elements that can affect a negotiation—not just the substantive, but also the psychological and emotional.

- Various tactics can be effective in various situations—but never get so caught up in a tactic that you lose your grace.

Chapter 14

NEGOTIATING TECHNIQUES

FOR LEADERS AND THEIR LAWYERS – MIDDLE AND ENDGAME GAMBITS

LAUNCHING!

Somewhere in the middle of a negotiation, human nature has the greatest impact on all of the available devices. Life experience and the negotiator's ability to recognize that the negotiation is a stage become important. Very often a quip, a joke, a war story, or other similar technique is just what is needed to reduce the tension. Sometimes the negotiator needs to create some levity or just change the atmosphere because he is doing too well. Sometimes a diversion is necessary because he is doing poorly and needs, in a gentle or joking manner, to take the opposition off stride. Think of a baseball game. Sometimes the batter steps out of the batter's box in order to break the pitcher's rhythm. These techniques cannot be learned from a book or an article. They must be observed and developed through social intercourse, drawing from all of the human situations we encounter, whether learning how to handle a bad joke at a cocktail party or how to deal with a colleague who just delivered a "drive-by insult" at the water cooler.

Many external influences can have an impact on a negotiation. For example, lunch is often the biggest rhythm-breaker and an almost necessary interruption. Therefore, the thoughtful negotiator must first decide whether or not he wants to break for lunch. Then, if there is going to be a lunch break, how to use it. Is it going to be social or will it be business? Will it be purely a lunch break or a working lunch? There are many considerations in connection with this potentially important break. Of course, there are also telephone breaks, bathroom breaks, interruptions by others, and so on. There can even be weather breaks. They occur when negotiations are being conducted during a bad or impending snowstorm or rainstorm. Another type of break might be

Chapter 14 | NEGOTIATING TECHNIQUES – FOR LEADERS AND THEIR LAWYERS – MIDDLE AND ENDGAME GAMBITS

referred to as the I-need-to-get-my-car-out-of-the-parking-lot-before-it-closes break or the I-have-to-be-at-the-airport-in-time-to-be-groped-by-security-and-make-the-plane break. Each one of these breaks can create tension as well as create a welcome (or unwelcome) diversion. Each has an impact on the rhythm of the negotiation, and may therefore be used effectively by the skilled negotiator to increase his leverage. In a very real sense, a negotiation is a chess game. Most moves are worth consideration; on the other hand, some are throwaways.

A good negotiator must maintain a high degree of intensity, regardless of how relaxed or joking he or she may appear during the proceedings. Accordingly, a good night's sleep is quite helpful. In addition, being physically as well as mentally fit is also very helpful. That is not to say that gold medalists will negotiate better than others; however, during the course of what may be a four-to-twenty-hour negotiation, or longer, perhaps over several days, the individual who is more mentally and physically fit will generally fare better. If nothing else, the fitter person will likely be more observant and better able to maintain focus throughout the negotiation. Losing focus—daydreaming—just proves the adage, "When you snooze, you lose."

Antagonism and compliment are important techniques that often arise in the middle stages of negotiations but, of course, can be used anytime. Generally speaking, it is unwise to antagonize the opposition. On the other hand, antagonism can be used to intimidate when the opposition is either ill-prepared or uninformed. However, antagonism should not be directed toward the other person. Ad hominem attacks are foolish and, frankly, bad form. Rather, it should be directed toward the opposition's statements, which is much more effective. By the same token, a well-placed compliment can often be disarming to the opposition, as well as making the compliment-giver look gracious. A compliment to the opposition need not go to the legal ability or validity of a position. It could be directed to the opposition's tie, blouse, or briefcase.

LAUNCHING!

Humility is another device (as well as a nice trait) which, when appropriately used, can be effective, as can the antithetical device of self-assurance. These devices can each disarm and/or intimidate the opposition when used by skilled negotiators.

Each negotiator must develop his own arsenal of devices and techniques. Not every device or technique will work with every negotiator. Each negotiator should work with those devices which fit his personality. The use of a device that does not fit the negotiator is as awkward and as obvious as wearing sneakers with a pinstripe suit. As negotiators develop as lawyers or businesspersons and evolve as human beings, they will recognize their strengths (and hopefully weaknesses) and use devices that fit those strengths. As each negotiator evolves, the arsenal of devices will change. Using devices that reflect feigned attitudes and feelings is not only going to be ineffective but will eventually be seen as dishonest (and most importantly, dishonest with oneself). The good negotiator may play act and oftentimes will need to do so. However, the good negotiator remains true to him or herself and never loses sight of the truth.

The Endgame

Some negotiations end with a bang, others with a whimper (apologies to T.S. Eliot). Often the pace of the negotiation has quickened in order to expedite resolution of the remaining issues. Most of us prefer to adjourn with a feeling of completion. The "completion complex" for most is quite strong. Skilled negotiators use it to their advantage. It is during this end-stage aspect of the negotiation that many seemingly small points may be too easily conceded by the negotiator who is tired or the client who is bored, or more concerned with returning home or catching a plane. It is during this aspect of the negotiation when skilled negotiators strengthen their resolve and take the time to win more points. Often, simple "stick-tuitiveness" wins points; the side with more resolve obtains better compromises. What should you do if your adversary

Chapter 14 | NEGOTIATING TECHNIQUES – FOR LEADERS AND THEIR LAWYERS – MIDDLE AND ENDGAME GAMBITS

with greater leverage insists on focusing on and winning every point as the deal approaches conclusion? Simply adjourn the meeting early. Find a reason! Postpone the deal. In the interim, the leverage may shift away from the side that is currently more powerful. Time heals many things and also creates the opportunity for leverage to shift, or at least adjust.

There are many other end-play gambits. When a negotiator senses his client is weakening in his resolve, the skilled negotiator simply ends the meeting by indicating that the balance of issues can be resolved by the negotiators via telephone. In this manner, weaknesses surfacing from the client can be concealed. On the other hand, a negotiator whose leverage is growing as the meeting is winding down can announce, in a non-offensive manner, that the meeting cannot adjourn and no one should leave until the deal is either completed or dies. This declaration can be softened and rationalized by indicating how difficult it will be to convene everyone in the future, or how difficult it will be for the negotiator to find time to meet again with his counterpart due to their schedules. Positions and strategies may change as a function of changing leverage. Understanding leverage is particularly important at the end of the meeting when important issues that could not be resolved earlier are revisited for resolution.

The decision to defer a difficult issue should always be analyzed. Deferring that issue until the late stages may give the skilled negotiator more information about the issue and a better understanding of the adversary, since by then he or she has discussed and resolved many issues already. With the additional time, the skilled negotiator will most likely find another way to compromise, given the earlier trade-offs. Moreover, the negotiator will have developed a clearer perception of the parties' relative leverage, in general, and with respect to the particular issue. On the other hand, deferral makes little sense in a scenario where the lapse of time may reduce leverage.

It is not uncommon for the skilled negotiator who has an overall

LAUNCHING!

weak position to nevertheless be able to win an important point at the end of the negotiation which could not have been won earlier. This can be accomplished through a variety of techniques, perhaps the simplest of which is to declare that since the other side won all of the other major issues, this last one has to go to his client or the deal is off! Sound risky? It is. But at this point, when the opposition has won so much, the bluff may easily work (assuming the bluff was worth taking) because the risk-reward analysis of the deal dying versus ceding one key point is simply against the other party who has already won most of the key points. If the bluff fails, a generous portion of humble pie will be served as you reverse your stand.

Another technique that can be introduced at any time in a negotiation is the premature yes. Prematurity is most effective when discussing a point you are prepared to concede. Offering an early yes to a point that you know full well you will concede later may be seen by the other side as a reason to believe you will be reasonable throughout the negotiation. It may reduce the other side's urge to play hardball with respect to all of the points it is prepared to concede.

The opposite technique—the premature no—can be equally effective. However, unlike the premature yes, the premature no is a bluff. You might offer a premature no so that a conciliatory yes offered later in the negotiation has more impact. These techniques (the premature yes and premature no) must be employed more with instinct than design. Of course, you must first be well prepared so you will understand which issues you will concede and which you will not.

Mutuality is so obvious it almost need not be addressed, but I would be remiss not to mention it. By virtue of the parties meeting to negotiate an agreement, they have the same goal—to get the deal done. In essence, both parties are there for the same reason. Why not suggest communal brainstorming to resolve some of the most difficult points? Mutuality suggests that you put the thorny issue(s) on the table early and say, "Let's throw this around and see if, together, we can find a solution that can work for both of us." For example, assume all of the

Chapter 14 | NEGOTIATING TECHNIQUES – FOR LEADERS AND THEIR LAWYERS – MIDDLE AND ENDGAME GAMBITS

parties know full well there is one issue that could create impasse. It is an issue for which neither party has so far been able to find a solution. This approach shows a willingness to listen to all sides and all views. It evidences an implicit willingness to compromise in order to solve the impasse.

Effective negotiators recognize when a particular issue cannot readily be resolved. On the other hand, the fact that an issue cannot be resolved before lunch does not mean it will not be resolvable before dinner. At the end of negotiations, a particularly difficult issue, together with other unresolved issues that have developed—when combined with the interpersonal glue that (hopefully) has developed—may all resolve as compromises emerge to reach agreement.

Just as a "no" is usually a "no, because," so too an impasse with respect to a particular issue does not mean it will remain an impasse forever. An impasse now can be compromised and solved later (when a solution to the "because" is found) if the parties work together to understand each other's needs.

What if one of the parties loses his composure, acts judgmentally, or launches a direct attack on another? Remember, don't personalize the negotiations—it's just business. Generally, we are only dealing with the resolution of commercial differences. Issues in a commercial context rarely involve a challenge to anyone's integrity or character. It's our ego that confuses the issues at hand with our integrity or character. Usually what we perceive as a trespass is simply due to misperception and misunderstanding. If the impasse focuses on something you said, don't assume you are being labeled a liar. Instead, consider the possibility that the other side misheard you or is misinterpreting what you said.

The Very End

In general, it is wise to make the other side feel that it has walked out with a win—that your adversary has done well, regardless of reality. It is always appropriate to give the other side a sense of success. This

LAUNCHING!

can be accomplished even though you have won virtually all of the important points. One way to do so is to offer cogent reasoning for the positions being taken by your client. Sometimes the reasoning may have to be as simplistic as corporate policy. Nevertheless, that reason is better than nothing (which may be perceived as arrogant), thereby removing the sting of what is, inherently, a harsh response to a particular issue. In addition, there are often many points that are quite unimportant to the negotiator that can be ceded to the other side. Sometimes, in the playacting of the negotiation, it is important for the negotiator to stand fast on a point that he knows he intends to concede (an offshoot of the premature no). In so doing, the other side feels it has obtained a victory if it only wins the point after prolonged discussion and argument. Another technique, similar to the last, to provide the other side with a sense of victory is to allow the negotiation of a particular point to be won by the other side only after the other side has made a detailed and lengthy presentation of the reasons why they should win the point. Then, only after much back and forth, does the negotiator agree thereby creating the sense of ceding the point solely on the basis of the merits.

Strategies and approaches to the endgame are myriad. Perhaps, however, the most important aspect of the endgame is the actual end. In other words, the way in which the goodbyes are made—the transition phrases used to maintain the glue for the next meeting or the follow-up telephone conversation. Regardless of how bitter or difficult a negotiation may have been, it is always appropriate to try to end the negotiation on an up note and with a sense of cordiality. This cannot always be done and should not always be done. However, for the most part, it is wise to end in such a manner unless there are good (non-ego-based) reasons not to do so. Remember, negotiations are composed of people, and human relations are critical to move deals forward.

The Documentation

It is not enough to negotiate well and leave the meeting after having

Chapter 14 | NEGOTIATING TECHNIQUES – FOR LEADERS AND THEIR LAWYERS – MIDDLE AND ENDGAME GAMBITS

won the negotiation, unless the fruits of that negotiation are properly reflected in the appropriate documentation. Some are quick to say they have no pride of authorship; on the other hand, others say they have little respect for those who have no pride of authorship. The only lasting memory of a negotiation is the written words that document that negotiation. Accordingly, the good negotiator should either be an excellent draftsperson or work with one. In fact, an often critical element of a negotiation is determining which side will draft the documentation. In general, the side that controls the drafting has the advantage. Many sub-issues, as well as sometimes major issues, arise as the paperwork is being drafted. Since these issues and sub-issues may not have been discussed or, even if discussed, left only partially resolved, the draftsperson has license to approach the un-discussed or unresolved issues from any perspective he desires. Obviously, the person drafting the document will lean the language toward his client. Drafting allows the writer to create nuances and inferences in favor of his client. In addition, some draftspersons will even draft the points won by the other side in as limiting a manner as possible, perhaps even undercutting them, as long as the points remain substantially intact. It is not uncommon for issues not addressed during the negotiation to be won simply by the side controlling the paperwork. While, of course, the other side may have comments and/or objections to approaches taken by the draftsperson, it is nevertheless true, although trite, that, "Once begun is half done." More often than not, much of what is initially drafted tends to remain as initially drafted.

Every negotiation constitutes a constantly changing mosaic of human emotion, drama, fact, legal issues, and a host of outside impacts such as airplane reservations, parking lot closures, personal events, and the like. In other words, a skilled negotiator is involved with all elements of life and is truly playing out a microcosm of life in all of its aspects. Accordingly, the skilled negotiator is one who understands the factual predicates as well as the legal issues involved in a deal, and has

LAUNCHING!

a good understanding of all of the human elements that constitute the drama of the negotiation.

To become skilled at negotiations, a degree in psychology is almost as important as a degree in the law, and both of those degrees should be coupled with an intensive understanding of the relevant business and industry segments which are the subject of the negotiation. A skilled negotiator is an actor, a director, a lawyer, and a psychologist all at once; oftentimes, depending upon the nature of the negotiation, the attorney-negotiator may also be called upon to be an engineer, an economist, or otherwise an expert in the business of the client.

PRACTICE POINTS

- Skilled negotiators constantly remain focused.

- Everything counts. Sometimes the seemingly trivial is important.

- Do not shy away from strong positions—if necessary, they can always be softened.

- Never lose your grace. Never attack the other side personally.

- No matter how well you did, never rub it in.

- Work hard to arrange for your side to draft the documentation—don't cede the drafting to your adversary.

Chapter 15
THE TRIPLE PLAY

LAUNCHING!

The underlying concepts and techniques that you must master to be an effective marketer (to enhance your personal brand) are the same concepts and techniques that you must master to become an effective leader and sharpen your negotiating skills. Why? Because effectiveness in each area requires enhancement of your interpersonal skills. When you become effective in one area, you will be effective in all three areas—a triple play!

The crucial skill at the root of all three areas is effective listening. Becoming a good listener is the bedrock skill necessary to be good at marketing, leading, or negotiating. Once we acquire the skill of good listening—and develop that skill in order to become a great listener—we can execute the triple play. Why? Because when others recognize we are listening to them—really listening with focus—they realize we are working to truly understand what they are saying. Once they realize we want to really get what they are saying, a bond of trust can begin to develop. We should always try to knit that bond, even if only to conduct a five-minute conversation. Effective listening will enhance all of our interpersonal relationships: family, business, and everything in between.

Let's examine why. Once we become effective as a listener, two other skills are almost automatically developed: focus and the ability to be in the present. A corollary skill that develops is the effective use of silence so we can listen and digest what we heard. All of these skills are relationship enhancers. As we achieve good listening skills, we immediately begin to develop good leadership skills. Why? Because until we learn how to listen, we cannot hear what our employees and/

Chapter 15 | THE TRIPLE PLAY

or colleagues are saying, and we cannot hear what the marketplace is trying to tell us.

Similarly, as we become good listeners, we instantly develop a key skill for marketing. What is more important for a marketer than the ability to hear and understand the needs and problems of his current or prospective client?

Think about it. Good listeners have learned how to focus and live in the present moment. As good listeners, we can easily apply the ten-second rule, the fifteen-second rule, and the 51 percent rule. These valuable rules will enhance all three skills.

The ten-second rule asks us to stop what we are doing and listen to anyone interrupting us (the surprise context): listen with focus and without interrupting for at least ten seconds. The fifteen-second rule asks us to listen to a subordinate or colleague reporting to us about a project or a recent event (it could be our child or spouse). In this non-surprise context, the rule asks us to turn our focus to them, not interrupt them, and listen intently for fifteen seconds.

Oh, how interminable ten or fifteen seconds can seem! Have you ever had to sit still—wait at a red light, wait in line, or otherwise be slowed down—when you felt under pressure, stressed, or anxious? If you have, then you know that until you learn to apply the ten-second rule and the fifteen-second rule in stressful situations, you haven't really learned them. You haven't mastered their teachings. But when you do learn to apply them during periods of anxiety, you will feel like a Zen master. You will have virtually automatically learned the underlying skill of compartmentalization.

Compartmentalization allows us to turn our full attention and focus from one matter to another. In fact, there is no such thing as successful multitasking. Who among us can concentrate on two things at the same time, giving them both their required due, and get them right? Multitasking should not be confused with simultaneity. Multitasking is moving from task to task (compartmentalizing one to deal with another) as part of working through a series of tasks. Life is seldom kind enough

LAUNCHING!

to allow us to work through a time-consuming errand or project from beginning to end without interruption. In fact, "alone time" seems to be getting more and more scarce. Isn't it amazing what just one good skill—listening—can beget?

We know good listening is a seminal skill in negotiating, and we can see how its mastery will improve our leadership skills. Now, let's give it a spin in the third leg of the triple play: marketing.

It should come as no surprise that so many marketing gurus trumpet the need to solve your prospect's problems instead of selling your "inventory of services." Those gurus urge marketers to be solvers, not sellers. Of course, in order to solve a client's problems, you must know and understand what the problems are. Common sense, therefore, dictates that you, the marketer, ask questions of your prospect or client and then allow the answer to be fully developed. To do so effectively, you must only do three things well to learn the client's needs: listen, ask questions, and listen again. That's what is required to aid the prospect in setting forth as much information as possible to enable you to better understand the client's problems.

Hence, the 51 percent rule. This rule urges marketers to listen—not speak—for at least 51 percent of a marketing presentation. Many marketing experts will suggest that when a marketer speaks for more than half the meeting, the likelihood of failure increases in proportion to the time in excess of 50 percent monopolized by the marketer.

Therefore, the concept of listening—as well as its corollary techniques and skills—are discussed and intertwined in this book and the two earlier books, which are part of this trilogy. When we master the techniques in any of the three areas—marketing, leadership, or negotiation—the likelihood is high that we can succeed in all of the areas.

The triple play is not about the baseball concept of getting all three outs in one play. Rather, it's more like those old-fashioned jukeboxes where you can choose three songs for twenty-five cents; kind of like getting three songs for the price of one. The price: the investment of time to be good at any of the three skill areas. The benefit: the triple play of becoming good at all three by becoming good at any one.

If you like the baseball analogy better than the jukebox analogy, let's consider a more positive baseball perspective. Envision the triple play as putting you on third base after rounding first and second—a stand-up triple (you didn't need to slide). Now, all you need to do is bring yourself home. I am rooting for you. So are all with whom you will come into contact—most of all your loved ones.

Let me know when you cross home plate.

P.S.: *Launching* completes a trilogy of books drawing upon my formal and informal studies and the lessons and techniques I have learned and successfully applied in my own business and personal life. *Launching*, together with my other books, *Listening* and *Leading*, fine tune skills and techniques I believe will take you to the next level in your business and personal development. If you are interested in reading *Listening* and *Leading*, you can find the books at www.amazon.com. I love your comments and feedback, so please feel free to contact me at jnewman@sillscummis.com.

NOTES

LAUNCHING!

NOTES

LAUNCHING!

NOTES

LAUNCHING!

NOTES

LAUNCHING!

NOTES

LAUNCHING!

NOTES

LAUNCHING!

www.ingramcontent.com/pod-product-compliance
Lightning Source LLC
Chambersburg PA
CBHW061440040426
42450CB00007B/1143